Sustainable
Ecosystems

and the built environment

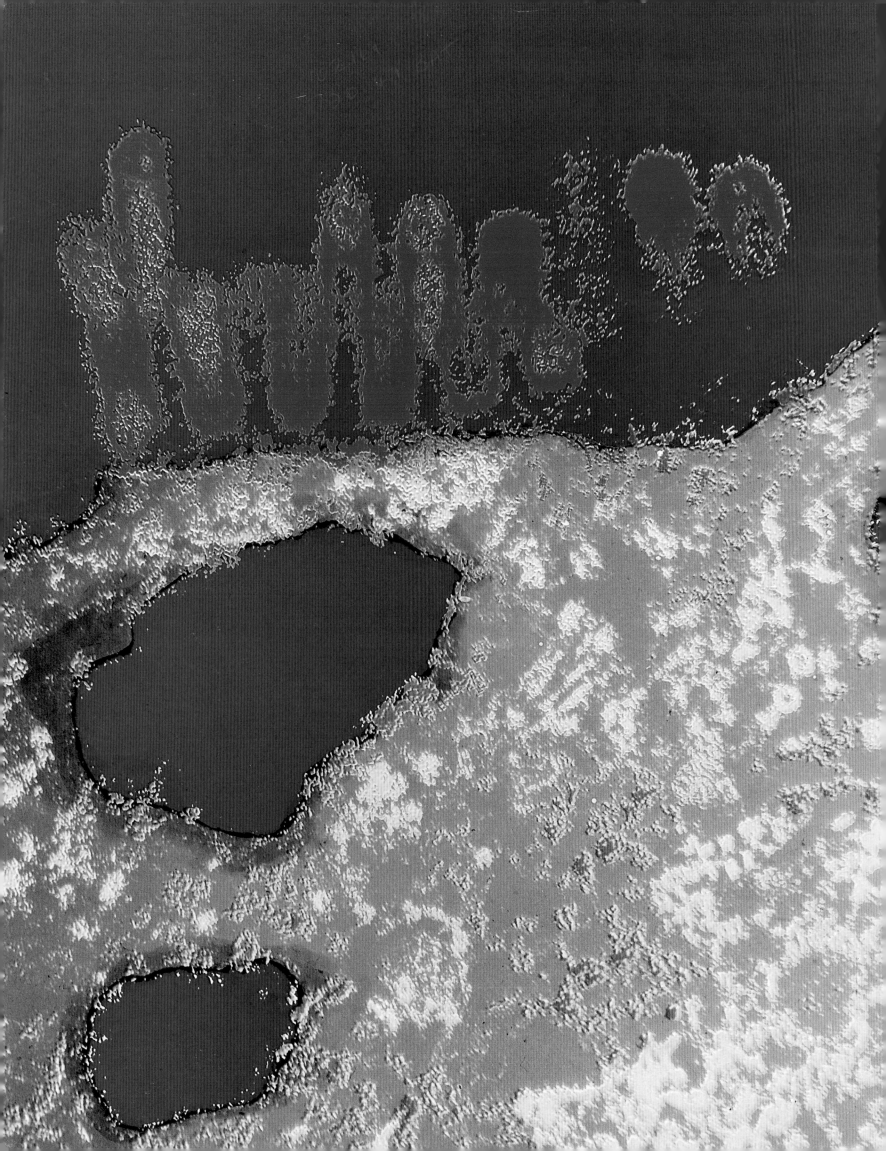

Sustainable Ecosystems

and the built environment

Guy Battle and Christopher McCarthy

WILEY-ACADEMY

Acknowledgments

Chris McCarthy and Guy Battle would like to thank all at Battle McCarthy.
They would also like to acknowledge the people who helped to write many of the
articles. Contributors are listed at the end of the articles that they helped to prepare.

All articles were published in issues of *Architectural Design* between 1994 and 1997.

Page 2: From *Landscape Sustained by Nature*, false-colour transmission
electron micrograph of a cell infected by influenza virus; courtesy of
Dr Gopal Multi/Science Photo Library

First published in Great Britain in 2001 by
WILEY-ACADEMY

a division of
JOHN WILEY & SONS LTD
Baffins Lane
Chichester
West Sussex PO19 1UD

ISBN 0-471-50007-0

Other Wiley Editorial Offices
New York • Weinheim • Brisbane • Singapore • Toronto

Layout and Prepress: ARTMEDIA PRESS Ltd, London

Printed and bound in Italy

contents

PREFACE

Guy Battle and Chris McCarthy founded the successful practice in 1993 and originated a creative design process, which combines an intuitive and analytical approach. This is based on Guy Battle's background in science and Chris McCarthy's background in art. The two first developed a working relationship with each other while working in the multidisciplinary environment of the engineering practice, Ove Arup and Partners. About 12 years ago, issues of sustainability started to become apparent and important in building design. In response, the two worked out ways to reduce the effects of climatic extremes on structures. While at Ove Arup, they worked on the environmental engineering for GSW Headquarters and the Marseille Town Hall. Guy and Chris realised that their work could influence architecture through an awareness of natural forces such as light, heat, sound and air movement. Their approach to design is to explore the mystery of the interaction between climate and structure rather than just approaching it as a problem to be resolved. Deciding that there was more to service engineering than mechanical systems, Guy and Chris started Battle McCarthy Consulting Engineers as a vehicle to deliver sustainable design.

Since its formation, the practice has worked on a range of projects throughout the UK and overseas with a diverse group of prestigious clients and world-class architects. Battle McCarthy has been and is currently involved with some of the most innovative green projects in the world. Projects have ranged in scale from single houses to office headquarters and university campuses to complete new urban settlements.

Through working on a wide range of projects over the years, Battle McCarthy has developed a proficiency in the analysis, design and installation of environmental building services systems. Battle McCarthy 's expertise encompasses a full range of integrated engineering and landscape services that play a significant role in their projects, from the design process, through construction to operation. The practice provides a holistic design approach to the services they provide, which include Environmental Engineering, Structural Engineering, Building Services Engineering, Landscape Design and Sustainable Masterplanning. This approach allows the engineers to gain a fully comprehensive understanding of the problem and then use the benefit of collective experience to focus on a workable solution. Battle McCarthy's successes are dependent upon the firm's comprehensive understanding of sustainable development as well as fostering the unique synergy of skills and experience within the practice.

Team working is an integral part of the process of multidisciplinary building design. Battle McCarthy can easily develop a successful relationship with various architects to create superior building designs. Battle McCarthy also cultivates partnerships with industry in order to allow newly developed technologies to reach a critical mass. In this way the practice are intermediaries between industry and architecture.

Battle McCarthy is also key player in researching and developing new technologies for the building professions. The practice is making important contributions to new developments and recent R & D (Reserch & Development) projects include double skin facades, building integrated wind towers, pre-engineered building systems, environmental design for museums, sustainable towers, intelligent building control systems and the creation of zero emission neighbourhoods. Battle McCarthy are not only driven by new highly technical solutions but also what can be learned from the climatic traditions and engineering solutions of the past.

Battle McCarthy value education and knowledge transfer and this is reflected by the directors' enthusiasm to teach. Guy Battle is the Environmental Tutor at the Architectural Association in London and teaches Environmental Building and Design at the Illinois Institute of Technology in Chicago. Chris McCarthy has been a senior visiting lecturer in Sculpture, Architecture and Interior Design, and Industrial Design at the Royal College of Art, and a visiting lecturer at the Imperial College, London University and Berlin University. Chris was also an external examiner to the University of Greenwich.

The work of Battle McCarthy is continuing to evolve through many R & D projects and the sustainable masterplanning of large schemes. The sustainable masterplan for redevelopment of the Elephant and Castle in central London has evolved out of the practice's plans for the Greenwich Millennium Village. This will have a far reaching impact as London acts as a major role model for urban redevelopment in other major cities throughout the world. The practice is also designing a new modular building technology for the Chinese government that will provide housing for more than a million people. The results of this significant project will also be applied to the Elephant and Castle redevelopment.

Battle McCarthy recently moved into a new headquarters based in Holborn, central London and a US office recently opened in Chicago. These places of work are a constant hive of activity and every day provides a new experience as the practice faces the challenges presented by numerous on-going projects. The Holborn office is set to become an R & D centre of excellence and professional point of convergence for ideas and innovations. The practice is bringing together leading architects, engineers and related professionals to discuss and develop new technologies and techniques.

Human Comfort

- Good daylight, views and air quality
- Suitable acoustics and insulation
- Good thermal control
- Suitable humidity control
- Good security and safety provision
- Good personal control
- High degree of adaptability

Design for change

- Simple and modular design to cope with incremental expansion
- Ease of re-routing services for changing functions and layout

Energy Consumption and CO_2 emissions.

- Maximising the use of free energies, such as daylight, sun, wind and temperature changes
- High levels of thermal insulation
- Reliable and suitable control systems
- Efficient building systems and plant
- Use of low cost fuels at off peak rates

Maximising usable space and minimising capital cost :

- Minimising plant area
- Minimising air distribution space requirements
- Maximising structural/service integration
- Removing the necessity for false ceilings

Minimise Operating costs by :

- Utilising durable materials
- Long life equipment
- Reliable and simple environmental control systems
- Good access for maintenance

Protect Ecology and Enhance Biodiversity :

- Integrating fauna and wildlife
- Considering green and blue conditions
- Collecting rainwater and recycling
- Effective waste management and recycling

"We are constantly seeking new structural engineering aesthetics driven by climatic form finding within a sustainable dimension"

Sustainable Future

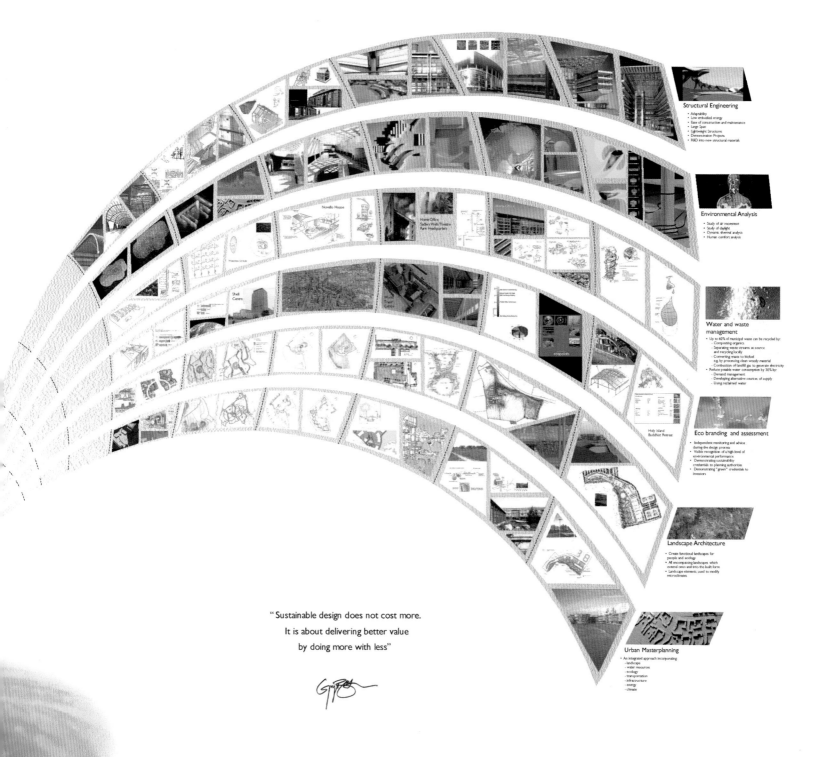

Structural Engineering

- Adaptability
- Low embodied energy
- Ease of construction and maintenance
- Large Span
- Lightweight structures
- Demonstration Projects
- R&D into new structural materials

Environmental Analysis

- Study of air movement
- Study of daylight
- Dynamic thermal analysis
- Human comfort analysis

Water and waste management

- Up to 60% of municipal waste can be recycled by:
  - Composting organics
  - Separating waste streams at source and recycling locally
  - Converting waste to biofuel e.g. by processing clean woody material
  - Combustion of landfill gas to generate electricity
- Reduce potable water consumption by 30% by:
  - Demand management
  - Developing alternative sources of supply
  - Using reclaimed water

Eco branding and assessment

- Independent monitoring and advice during the design process
- Visible recognition of a high level of environmental performance
- Demonstrating sustainability credentials to planning authorities
- Demonstrating "green" credentials to investors

Landscape Architecture

- Create functional landscapes for people and ecology
- All encompassing landscapes which extend onto and into the built form
- Landscape elements used to modify microclimates

Urban Masterplanning

- An integrated approach incorporating
  - landscape
  - water resources
  - ecology
  - transportation
  - infrastructure
  - energy
  - climate

"Sustainable design does not cost more.
It is about delivering better value
by doing more with less"

INTRODUCTION

Throughout history, engineers have produced some of the finest testaments to human achievement. We still marvel at accomplishments like the Eiffel Tower, the Hoover Dam and more recently, the Channel Tunnel and space technology. The greatest engineering successes of our civilisation are innovations that have universal value, and were developed in direct response to real needs: transportation systems, communication networks, flood and sewage control strategies, and other urban infrastructures.

At this crucial turning point in the evolution of our species, with the new global culture that has been emerging since the latter part of the twentieh century, the need for extensive solutions to global problems is growing exponentially as populations increase. The role of the engineer has never been so evidential, and engineering has become one of the most exciting professions. The great visions that will significantly improve our lives require the solutions found through this fascinating vocation.

Most important is the engineer's ability to respond to change. The profession is acutely aware of the mounting dilemmas that we must deal with as a global culture. While society is drunk on consumerism, oblivious to the accumulated entropy that threatens to deteriorate into chaos, engineers are attempting to clean up after the party, vigilantly searching for solutions.

Quite often, tremendous solutions will cause unexpected problems. The engineer can potentially make more visual impact on the world than the most powerful filmmaker, can heal more people than the finest hospital, but can also kill more people than the largest army. Unfortunately, engineering has made an inconceivable impact on the surface of the planet through disasters like the demise of the Aral Sea and the ecological horrors of the Gulf War.

The job of the engineer is therefore not an easy one, involving huge responsibilities and high expectations. A good engineer must make informed decisions and will have to live by them. There is a large degree of conflict and stress involved in providing creative answers to complex challenges, and yet we must concentrate on a problem until it has transmuted into a solution. Like Kamikaze pilots, we hone in on a target and attack it with full force. This engagement of confrontation pushes the limits and sometimes rattles people's cages along the way.

Engineering is about calculated risks and thus requires a surplus of information – the more complexity the better. This offers an opportunity for the widest variety of intelligent and practical solutions. Unlike scientists, engineers do not experiment with this information, but instead, apply science for real human needs. While mechanics take things apart and put them back together, engineers will look at the elements in detail and put them back together differently to make them better. In the universe of humanity, the mind of the engineer is analogous to a black hole that envelops all information in order to produce the 'big bang' of a perfect universal solution on the other side.

Although our trade is market driven, it remains alert, refusing to fall into the trap of fat-cat lethargy. Our aim is clear: a better life for all. Like a big friendly giant with an ear to the ground, the engineer can hear from miles around, collecting and deciphering the dreams of others, and we have the capacity to realise these dreams.

Now that the days of conventional engineering are over, we have to juggle roles ranging from businessman to social engineer. We have to consider supply-chain management, sustainability issues, industrialised housing, economics, governance, employment and facility management. Engineers must understand both functional art and science, and through this, orchestrate, manage, enthuse, innovate and engage on many levels. We must make our profession more publicly accessible, taking our intelligence to new levels of interaction and act as role models for others. We must actively collaborate with all interested parties in an effort provide solutions whether it is with architects, manufacturers, communities, scientists or governments.

It is surprising then that the engineering profession is not more revered in our society. But engineering is not glamorous. Perhaps this is because image is so often chosen over function. While architecture is seen as a vocation, its kudos protected and well-defined, when an engineer dies, he is usually forgotten. However, his work continues to live on and the lack of signification is perhaps a blessing in disguise, bypassing the limitations of a socially imposed self-importance.

How then does one define Battle McCarthy? Who are we? We are everywhere, like air, both invisible and vital to the built environment. The practice consists of many creative people who are unafraid of challenges, including leading senior engineers, landscape architects and in-house architects, working in collaboration with eminent scientists and ecologists. This assortment of specialists is working together to provide fast solutions that work. Over the years, our visionary engineering has established us as leaders in environmental design, defining an entirely new field of architectural engineering. We have explored new spheres of human interface with our surroundings, and have acquired a true and thorough understanding of the effects of ecology and climate on architecture.

The articles in this book reflect this creativity and cover all elements of our multidisciplinary design and engineering approach to date, from the aesthetics of composite detailing in structural engineering, to the subtle effects of climatic perception on human behaviour. They were written for *Architectural Design* at various points in time, when the practice was confronting the different issues of the day. Included are details of some of the many projects on which the company has worked, as well as practical explanations of the science and art that underlies our approach to the discipline of environmental-building engineering. The book constitutes a grand summary of the developments made by the practice, concluding with the final article, which describes a project reflecting the culmination of years of design research, development and application. We now stand on the precipice of the future, reinventing ourselves once again for a brave new world of urban engineering.

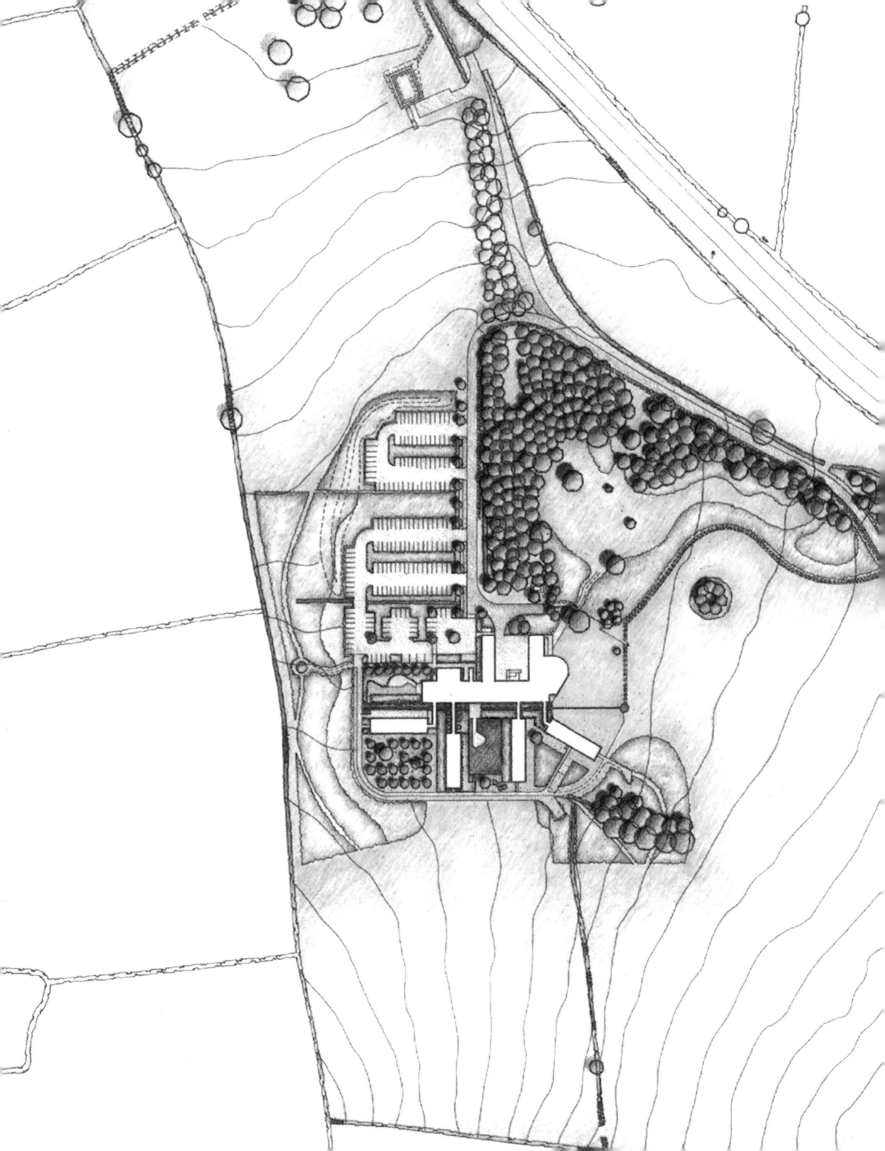

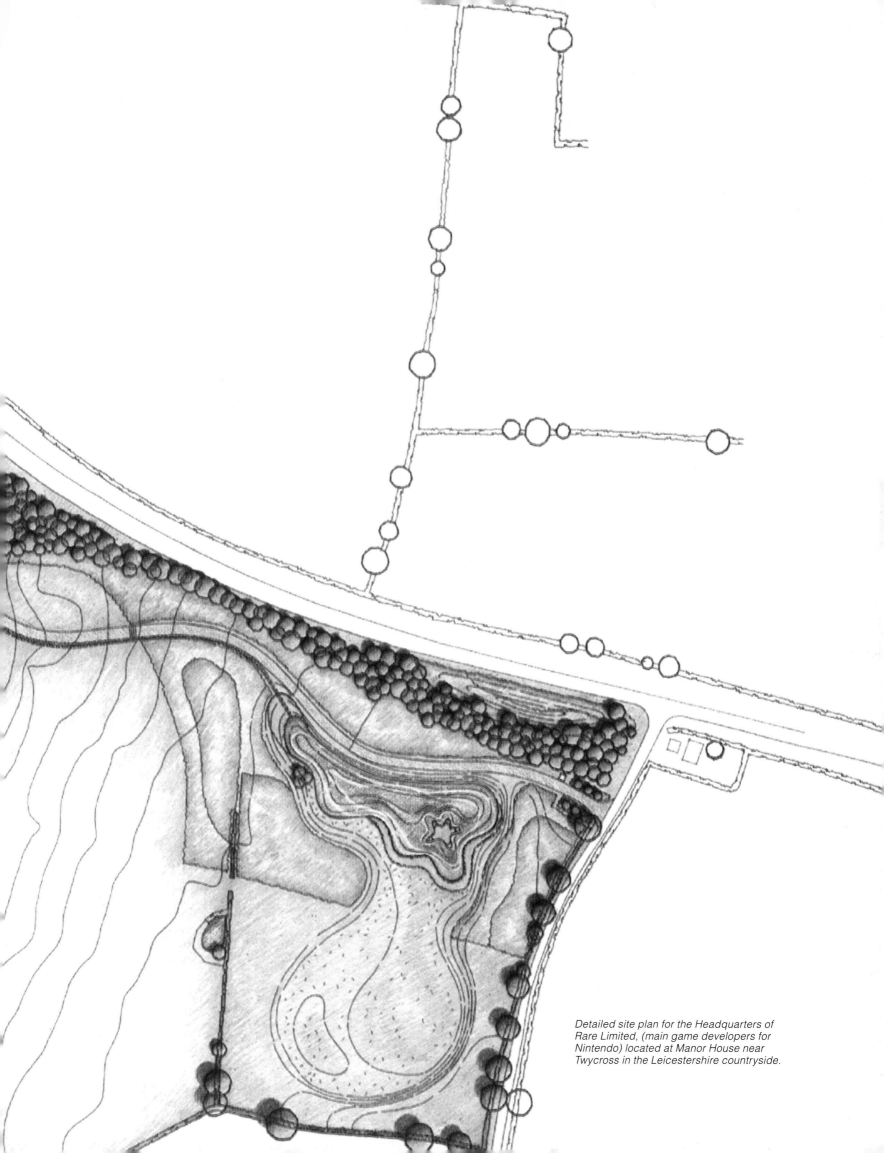

Detailed site plan for the Headquarters of Rare Limited, (main game developers for Nintendo) located at Manor House near Twycross in the Leicestershire countryside.

STRUCTURES RENEWED DIALOGUE WITH CLIMATIC FORCES

The Gothic pioneer masons and carpenters of the 13th century developed new ways of distributing weight, dispensing with the ponderous mass of Romanesque masonry, thus assisting architecture to soar up elegantly with the penetration of daylight. By definition they were the first building engineers. Through trial and error, but with absolute confidence in their imaginations (making calculations subservient), the Gothic structural masters were able to attempt and develop audacious technical departures. In no other period has the tie between material form and natural forces been so evident.

It was a special characteristic of these first building engineers that they were also sculptors. As such, they were creative, visually confident and visually critical: their imagination and skills at work on every part of the building, developing natural forms into their structural and environmental analysis and design, and even converting a water spout into an amusing or grotesque gargoyle. In light of these observations the progress achieved by these engineers seemed to be truly miraculous. They were the real forerunners of modern high technology, replacing an equilibrium achieved by heavy masses of masonry with an equilibrium of forces created by the interplay of thrust and counter-thrust of slender ribs to be filled with light.

This engineering revolution developed into a tradition of the natural combination of gravity and climatic forces in one form; a tradition which persisted through the Gothic, Renaissance and Baroque periods until the advent of the Industrial Revolution.

It was the 'Mono Task' efficiency requirements of the Industrial Revolution which isolated structural engineering from climatic forces. This view of technology, further developed throughout the 19th and 20th centuries, is responsible for the unsatisfactorily fragmented situation of today. Valuable energy resources are expended on overcoming the climatic shortcomings of ill proportioned structures to achieve the desired internal comfort for the user of the building. However, the architectural profession has more recently gained access to advanced solar and air flow computer modelling facilities to complement the stress and strain computer software already in use. The most fascinating results may be achieved by combining this technology with the design approach of medieval master craftsmen which are yet to be experienced.

Engineering natural forces: In natural structures, forces act directly on the form, so that it is a direct response to force. In his remarkable treatise *On Growth and Form* published in 1917, D'Arcy Thompson explored the functional aspect of organic growth. He concluded that the growth of the skeletal form is to a very large extent brought about by the body's mechanical forces. His theory is illustrated by individual bones eg the hip joint, manifesting themselves as a diagram or a reflected image of the mechanical stresses explained by an idealised finite stress analysis.

Perhaps the most vivid and elementary example of forces generating form in nature occurs during the growth and movement of clouds. Clouds are ever-changing, every second of the day. As thermal effects change, cloud structure reforms to achieve equilibrium with the new forces. Natural structures and forms are evolved in a constant process of adaptation. Those systems which do not adapt, disappear. Man-made constructive growths of form, such as in structural engineering interpret the forces mathematically; the engineer must be able to assess all the forces involved, many of which may not be apparent but which act upon the structure (and indeed originate from within it). Those forces not accounted for do not disappear but remain influential, constantly demanding that the structure should change to accommodate them. For example, the penetration of solar gain and resultant overheating of a structure leads to the growth of shading in the form of overhangs and shaped columns. In the most general terms, the problem facing the engineer has always been to measure these forces and establish a method by which each force is accommodated within one form, as well as assessing the performance of the structure's response to the forces.

Interaction between natural forces, structure and materials: For a long time structural forms have been dominated by gravity. In this view the art of structural engineering has appeared to be solely associated with structural acrobatics to cope with gravity. We now understand that we live in a pluralist world where climatic molecular and atomic forces are to be incorporated within the field of structural design.

Charles Darwin suggested that survival always

depends upon the capacity to adapt to changing circumstances. His theory holds true for structural engineering: a prediction for the future based upon a natural evolution, a reasoned and reasonable extension of ancestral trends, and the need to satisfy dynamically changing definitions of building performance and needs. Important in this strategy is the realisation that there is an established relationship between form and physical and climatic forces. It is also important that the forces are seen to exist as a series of interacting elements and are not isolated. Therefore a change in any force will naturally affect the whole.

The natural forces which a structure is to be designed for may be broken down into broad categories: gravity; interior ventilation; wind; sound; light; solar radiation; solar absorption. The natural forces can now be analysed and illustrated by a host of most advanced techniques, handed down from the masters of today's high tech industries.

Given a set of physical and climatic forces, how can we generate a single structural form which will be appropriate to all of them, and once we have established the structural form, how can we assess the aesthetic forces which arise from within it?

It is only through designing with the knowledge and feeling of a technical artist that the individual will be able to interpret the purpose of all these forces and how they may be best fulfilled within one eventual structural form.

Gravity: Perhaps the simplest device for illustrating gravitational force is by hanging like a chain a number of weights from a length of string. Structural engineers and architects alike have in the past used this analogue to generate the most appropriate geometry of a structure for a particular gravity load case.

Gaudi used the analogue of weights suspended from trees to generate the most appropriate form in stone. He constructed upside-down wire model analogues in which wires represented the columns and hanging bags of lead shot represented the eventual compressing loads. Another analogue of forces generating a form is that of a soap bubble under varying pressures and boundary conditions, the eventual form being that whereby minimum surface tension is achieved. This analogue is the principal means for 'form finding' air supported structures.

The anticlastic surfaces of tent structures are inherently 'voluminous' and 'multidirectional'. The contours of stress distribution were originally demonstrated with the use of nylon stockings, but now they may be illustrated with the visual aids of computer analysis.

A theorem by AGM Michelle made it possible to generate the cantilever form of the least-weight structure uniquely from a specification of the form. The theorem shows that all the members of

the least-weight structure must lie on one of the two families of orthogonal curves, the compression curve on one curve, and the tension on the other. The finite element analytical three-dimensional computer analysis now available provides an effective structural laboratory where one may add and subtract materials from a structural form at will until all the materials are working at the ultimate capacity, and thus achieve the required strength and stiffness for the least amount of material.

Wind forces: As structures become taller and lighter, wind load design becomes a more significant factor for the design of structures than gravity. Not surprisingly the Eiffel Tower grows from the ground as a giant multidirectional cantilever. With the need for taller chimneys, intensive research into dynamic wind flows around objects was intensified with the aid of aeronautical wind tunnel tests. Today, high-rise buildings are as common in wind tunnel test facilities as racing cars and aeroplanes.

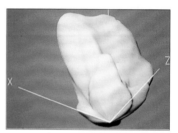

The study of wind performance around structures goes beyond the need to predict wind dynamic forces on the proposed structure. It has led to a better understanding of wind pressures around the building for the comfort of pedestrians at ground level.

Andrew Wright of Richard Rogers Partnership has used the structural form to accelerate the wind between building block and the service core, where wind turbines are positioned to generate power for an energy self sufficient office block. A similar principle is presently being pursued by Kohn Pederson Fox for the Redevelopment of the Martini Tower in Brussels.

Wind towers have been used for ventilation for the last 3000 years, as is evident in natural construction such as termite hills. Dr Ken Yeang is presently leading research and development on ventilating high rise towers with minor wind scopes. Traditionally the understanding of wind around an object was demonstrated with wind tunnel tests. More recently, wind computer modelling is providing more realistic simulation. These design tools will pioneer new departures in architectural form from the shapes of tower blocks to the emergence of wind tower and roof scope incorporating wind power generators.

Micro convection forces: The reason for internal air flow is due to natural convection currents caused by differential temperature or because of different air pressures at different openings to the outside. These forces may be modelled by computer fluid dynamic software or by physical thermal salt model tests used to predict thermal differentials and air movement. This analysis and testing is particularly important for assessing not

FROM ABOVE: Marseilles, 1994. *Photograph: William Alsop; computer simulation of light; computer simulation of thermal air flow; OPPOSITE: Heaven and Earth 1992, Video installation detail, 1993/94 Whitechapel Gallery Exhibition. Photograph: Kira Perov*

only ventilation flow but also fire and smoke spread to achieve safer buildings. These techniques were utilised by Willem Neutelings during the design development of the ABN-AMRO Bank Headquarters Building Proposal for Amsterdam.

Sound: The periodic motion of molecules is a form of energy called sound. If two objects are brought into contact, then some of the more intense motion of one object will be transferred to the other object. The molecules must be close to each other in order to collide. Since in air the molecules are far apart, air is not a good conductor of sound, compared to water or solid objects, and a vacuum allows no conduction of sound at all. Sound is generated through the air, and interacts with the surface of structural materials in a number of different ways: transmittance; absorption; reflection. The type of interaction that will occur is not only a function of materials but also the wavelength and frequency of the sound. The passage or sound may be analysed with the aid of computer simulation or physical sound model tests. Nick Thompson and Ljiljana Blagojevic of RHWL collaborated closely with Arup acoustics in sculpting the auditorium 'bowl' and roof to generate the final structural form of the Manchester concert hall which is presently under construction.

Force of light: The form of a structure is known to us primarily by the way it reflects light. Sensitive designs have always take into account that what we see is a consequence of how the light falls on the structure. Computer simulation generates light controls which vary as window positions alter and the angle of reflection changes. Computer modelling generates a three-dimensional interpretation of the sea of light which may be sculpted by external condition until the desired effect is achieved. Richard Jobson of Plincke Leaman & Browning has developed the form of each building of the D' Hautree School Project in Jersey in response to the daylight requirements of each specific function contained within. The classroom roofs, for example are modelled to distribute *even* daylight throughout the space, which avoids the situation where lights are switched on due to variation of light levels.

Force of solar radiation: For part of the year the sun is our friend and for part of the year it is our enemy. People used to worship the sun as a god because they understood how much life depended on it.

The sun is a huge 25M °C fusion reactor in which light atoms are fused into heavy atoms and in the process energy is released. The amount and composition of radiation reaching the earth's surface depends upon the angle which it strikes and the composition of our atmosphere.

The transmission of radiation is affected by the nature of the materials with which it interacts. Some materials are transparent to infra-red,

others absorb it and others are opaque to it. The objective of shading devices is either to reflect radiation or to absorb it and re-radiate away from the structure. To simulate shade, shadows and solar penetration, structural forms may be placed within a heliodon. This apparatus is used to simulate the shadow created by the structure at a particular point on the earth's surface, at any time of year.

Evolution of shading device: 'The solar control device has to be on the outside of the building, an element of the facade, an element of architecture. And because this device is so important as part of our architecture, it may develop into as characteristic form as the doric column.' Marcel Breuer.

Once the maximum and minimum solar angles onto the facade are determined, together with a specification for the reflection and penetration of solar radiation throughout the seasons, the types of solar shading devices may be examined in a trial and error process, including: fixed horizontal shades; fixed vertical screens; movable horizontal louvres; movable vertical blinds or fins.

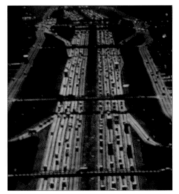

In an effort to protect the external shades from the extreme effects of the climate a second glazed facade may be erected. This generates a solar updraught. This may then be used to draw air from the building, and thus aid cross ventilation, especially for high rise buildings. This is demonstrated in the proposed GSW Headquarters Building by Sauerbruch and Hutton, for which thermal analysis computer programmes (CFD) were used to simulate the thermal flue in action and show the thermal temperature variation.

Thermal mass: Heavyweight structures feel cool on hot summer days because they act as a thermal store. At night, they give up their heat by convection to the cool night air and by radiation to the cold outer atmosphere at absolute zero – thus 'recharging' their heat sink capability for the next day.

David Emond of RH Partnership has developed the Ionica Headquarters Building which maximises the thermal mass of the concrete slabs, with the passage of air supply through the hollow cores of standard precast concrete floor slabs to provide a source of free summer cooling during mid season and summer periods.

Thermal resistance: The opposition of materials to the flow of heat by conduction, convection and radiation is called thermal resistance measured largely as a function of the number and size of air spaces that they contain. This is commonly known as the insulative properties of materials. The high performance insulative materials developed for space suits have insulative properties equivalent to meters of concrete. However, under hot and cold dynamic conditions, 120mm of concrete may

FROM ABOVE: Simultaneous response by shoal of hatchet fish; Los Angeles Freeway, 1994; Maurice Brennan Energies in Ebullition

appear to have a greater resistance than 10mm of timber. This is due to the time lag of the concrete mass heating up. The 'insulating' effects of mass is most beneficial in hot dry climates during the summer. This effect is not helpful in humid climates where the temperature remains constant.

Interpretation of climatic forces: Paul Cézanne, reacted against the lack of structure in the work of the impressionists and declared his intention to make impressionism into 'something solid and durable'. Cézanne's rigorous analysis of structure has made him one of the fathers of modern art, an inspiration to abstract artists through his pains-taking analysis of colour which replaced light and shade as his means of modelling.

It is fascinating studying an artist at work. One may observe the whirl of the brush in a flashing stroke across the canvas or the gouging of the clay to form beautiful works of art. Whether or not the final result of such energy is recognisable image, it is the process itself which becomes a work of art – unlike traditional artists of the pre-twentieth century. Such contemporary artists are not preoccupied with a pictorial physical image but by balance of sensations and images: motion/stability, strength/weakness, tension/strain, light/dark, hot/cold, noise/silence; indeed, the main ingredients of engineering. There is a mystical quality in abstract art which is difficult to explain but so true to interpretations of natural forces.

Duithuit, in the catalogue of an exhibition of paintings by Riopelle in 1945, wrote of 'the work of this French-Canadian painter – a kind of aerial impressionism, extremely fickle, adapting its own fury to the capacity of the executor, and the ruling of its own in powerful rhythms. Most painters desire to be a force of nature integrated into nature and to lose control in order to gain a certain explosive vigour, a constant source of masterpieces'. Similarly this energising can be applied to an interpretation of natural forces effecting in architecture. We should first channel our understanding of the interaction of structural form with physical and climatic forces on paper as force and flow diagrams expressing technical performance.

There are many ways of expressing the interaction of structural materials and form with physical and climatic forces in all the surging seas of contemporary searching towards meaningful diagrammatic expression. When collaborating with the architect Will Alsop on the Marseilles Hotel du Départment, although part of Ove Arup Partnership we did not necessarily 'see' environmental performance of the structure completely in our minds before beginning to sketch environ-

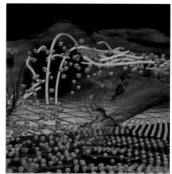

mental force diagrams or to model structural form with Will Alsop; nor was an image conceived of a structured environment which had only to be sketched on paper with a pencil, or visualised electrical technics. Generally, a sense of Alsop's intentions was the starting point, with the environment illustrated by a series of paintings, but it was not possible to define clearly and predict a conclusion without proceeding with a degree of analytical trial and error.

The engineer's perception of structural form and orientation, and the image of environmental performance, grows with the architect's vision; from the first pencil stroke on the paper to the last in an organised manner, one touch demanding another. Sketching an image of the predicted environmental performance of a structure is in some ways an act of three-dimensional elimination, in that one sets up a structural model, a column here and an exposed slab overhang there, making adjust-ments and correcting relationships as one works to eliminate and sketch over irritations of poor daylight penetration, lack of thermal mass, lack of cross-ventilation due to faulty composition and indecisive structural form and materials, until the image of an environ-mentally efficient structural form seems complete and whole.

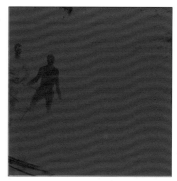

We are, at this moment in the world's history, part of a privileged elite with an unparalleled opportunity to develop renewed interpreta-tions of natural forces associated with building physics. There are thousands of climatic and atmospheric laboratories and computer analytical programmes which are readily available to be explored with universities, and consultants are dedicated to analysing and testing physical and climatic performance with form and ready to communicate this. The similar minded scientists and artists should be encour-aged to participate in the realisation of architec-ture's image in collaborative efforts to create form from formless matter of mutual physical and climatic stimulation in the spirit of cooperation in coordinating differences. One can only imagine what Gaudi would have created beyond the hanging chain analysis if computational physical and climatic computer and laboratory facilities of today were made available as he was modelling the Guell Chapel in Barcelona.

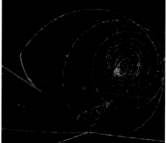

The authors wish to acknowledge the contribution made by Maurice Brennan to this article.

FROM ABOVE: Computer simulation of air movement inside a cloud; The Capsiz-ing of Garthsnaid September 1911; vapour trails after high speed particle collision

GENESIS OF NATURAL FORCES

Higher technology architectural visions may go beyond the innovative application of known materials and technologies from other industries associated with the hardware of the industrial past. They should pursue the scientific revolution in the field of computer simulation of physical and environmental forces.

Technology transfer associated with our construction industry is, for example, less about taking the form and materials of an aeroplane, pulling off its wing and renaming it a house. It is more to do with using the air flow computer simulation programmes generated by the aircraft industry to predict the enhancement of natural ventilation with the aid of high level openings known as 'wind towers'. The efforts of such analysis may result in a form and use of materials which do not look 'high-tech' as we have come to know it, perhaps seem less clever, but certainly will be understood and appreciated as a more intelligent one.

The most decisive factors in 'form finding' a structure are involved with the interaction of materials with natural forces of gravity, wind, solar, light, sound, temperature and air movement: a materialisation of stresses following; strain yielding; deflection occurring; light being reflected and diffused; solar radiation being absorbed and re-radiated; air molecules moving from high to low pressure sources; sound being deflected and then absorbed, and so on.

Architecture has always been fired by the challenging comprehension of the interaction of materials with natural forces, whether it is dealing with a single natural force or many within a single form: *gravity* – from the construction of Stonehenge to the cantilever pylon of Calatrava's bridge for Seville; *wind* – from the aerodynamic shaping of Viking ships to Alsop's response to the mistral winds experienced by the Hotel du Departement for Marseilles; *solar* – from the Palm House of Kew to the latest solar collector glazing presently being developed by BP; *light* – from the dynamic light control devices for the central hall of La Villette to the science fiction satellite daylight reflectors which will orbit the globe providing endless daylight to all major centres of population; *temperature* – from the evaporative cooling techniques optimised by Alhambra's water features to the heat store techniques optimised by the Hong Kong Bank's major subterranean

water tunnel to the sea; *air movement* – from the muskrats tunnelling technique which enhance natural ventilation due the air pressure differences induced by the low entrance and the high exit to the enormous cooling towers which grow from our landscape; *sound* – from Aalto's sound boxes to the dynamic structural form and acoustic space of the Manchester Concert Hall. Whatever our excuse, the domination of natural forces remains part of the human record.

Evolution of our understanding of natural forces interaction with materials: Given a set of natural forces, how may we form find with the sensitivity towards the quality inherent in structural materials which will eventually create an enclosure to the environmental comfort and satisfaction of the occupier with the minimum dependence upon valuable energy sources.

Like designers before him, Antonio Gaudi used hanging chain modelling techniques as a means of generating the primary structural form of the Guell Chapel in Barcelona. Experimenting with a series of upside-down wire models, in which the wires stood for columns and the attached bags of lead shot stood for the self-weight of the roof, Gaudi was able to form find an appropriate gravitational form. The unrestrained mechanism was free to move as the applied loads were varied until the final form within envelope of applied load fulfilled the design requirement. The form was then mapped out, inverted and finally built in stone.

This 'gravitational' sculptor's apparatus for generative form from physical forces can now be more accurately and rapidly achieved by computer form finding analysis such as the Fablon programme developed by Alistair Day and Terence Haslett of Arup. The finite element analysis computer programmes developed by the design studios of the manufacturing industry for measuring and understanding stress and strain flow intensity through structural components for all types of load cases, have now become a fundamental tool for structural analysis from the analysis of steel castings to concrete flat slabs of Owen William's Boots Factory and to Nervi largespan shell structures. In addition to the development of computational means of 'sculpting' physical forces, engineers have also provided architects with means of simulating the forces of light, sound, temperature and air movement with the use of advanced computer software handed

Initialised form

down by the aerospace industries.

This article aims to illustrate and demonstrate the potential use of computer simulation of natural forces on form based upon a hypothetical enclosure. The conception of the volume has been defined by a group of four 70m-diameter spheres contained within a single membrane. It has also been assumed that the structure is buoyant and is floating at sea on the equator. Admittedly the complexity of the brief for designing a building requires many forces other than natural forces such as function, social, economic and psychological forces. However, like Gaudi's gravitational experiments before us, the objective of this abstract demonstration is not to design a building but to create prototypes which demonstrate the architectural potential of using the latest computer software appliances for the simulation of natural forces which are waiting to be exploited for whatever the building type and its global location. The objective of the exercise is to form find a common structural enclosure where each of the natural forces may be co-ordinated without compromising its individual qualities. To solve this mystery, we first need to simulate, in as abstract a manner as possible, the force intensity of each of the primary natural forces and then try and reshape the structure in response to moderating these individual abstract forces. This process revealed three structural forms in harmony with the three primary forces of gravity, air molecular behaviour and radiation then by fusion single form was generated.

Sixteen forms are sought by the individual forces. To simplify the assessment, these were grouped under three types of forces: mechanical forces; radiation forces; air molecule forces. From these merged force diagrams, three new forms were established by co-ordinating the differences without eliminating the individual quality of each force. The only geometrical restraint was that the plan shape at the water level had to remain unchanged. The mechanical forces seek a pyramidal shape with a single peak and catinary sides. To minimise radiation gain the plan area should be minimised leading to straightening up

of the sides with the flat roof. However, to ensure that good air movement is maintained, a number of high points are required. These new forms were then fused together by superimposing the computational forms by engineering judgement. The optimum form was thus generated. However, with more time and resources this composition of materials and form could have been extended to include more forces, and have been reviewed and assessed by computational 'random experience', whereby a variety of material passive and active properties could have been introduced into the analysis.

'One's vision is only as good as one's ability to justify that vision.' This design process was founded upon the intuitive form finding skill and knowledge of the design team's interpretation of the computer simulations. This analytical form finding approach, of investigating the theoretical form sought by each natural force, created a family of identifiable abstract forms into a network of compositions. These compositions were then merged by a sequence geometrical alignment towards an ideal composition.

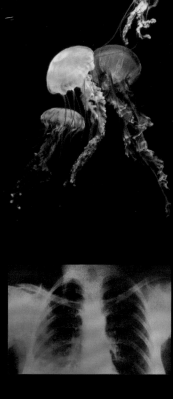

Together with the inevitable conflicts between the demands of each force, an understanding of each natural force, performance geometry and materials, became the inspiration for architectural forms in terms of space, density and radiation. This approach may be the 'high-tech' architecture of the 90s. Computational simulation of natural forces is available and affordable. Architects may use such tools to expand their interpretation of natural forces with form. The engineering vocabulary of the architectural form of these abstract computer simulations does not claim to pose architectural solutions for the built form but claims to be a more realistic representation for predicting the future physical and environmental performance of the architecture than any artist's impression submitted in a planning submission.

The authors wish to thank Barnaby Gunning for his contribution to this article.

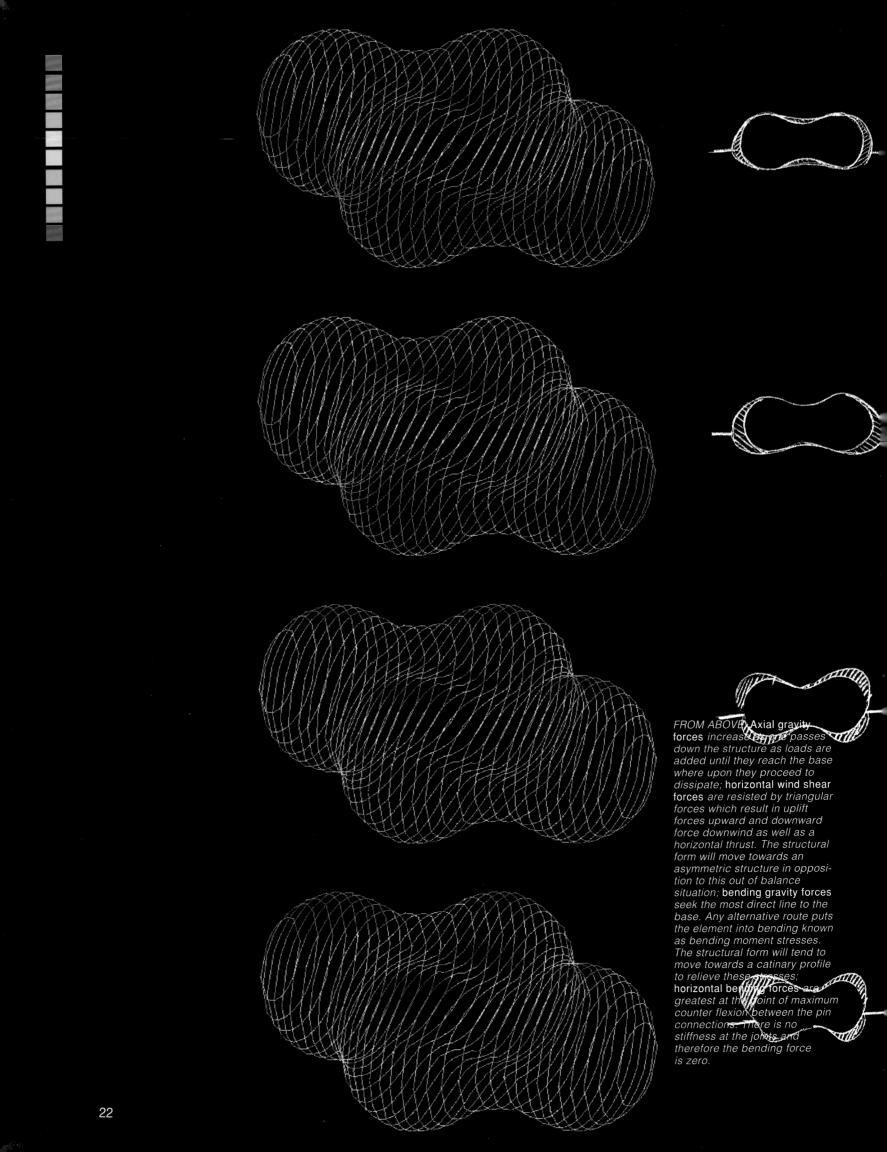

FROM ABOVE: Axial gravity
forces *increase as one passes
down the structure as loads are
added until they reach the base
where upon they proceed to
dissipate;* horizontal wind shear
forces *are resisted by triangular
forces which result in uplift
forces upward and downward
force downwind as well as a
horizontal thrust. The structural
form will move towards an
asymmetric structure in opposition to this out of balance
situation;* bending gravity forces
*seek the most direct line to the
base. Any alternative route puts
the element into bending known
as bending moment stresses.
The structural form will tend to
move towards a catinary profile
to relieve these stresses;*
horizontal bending forces *are
greatest at the point of maximum
counter flexion between the pin
connections. There is no
stiffness at the joints and
therefore the bending force
is zero.*

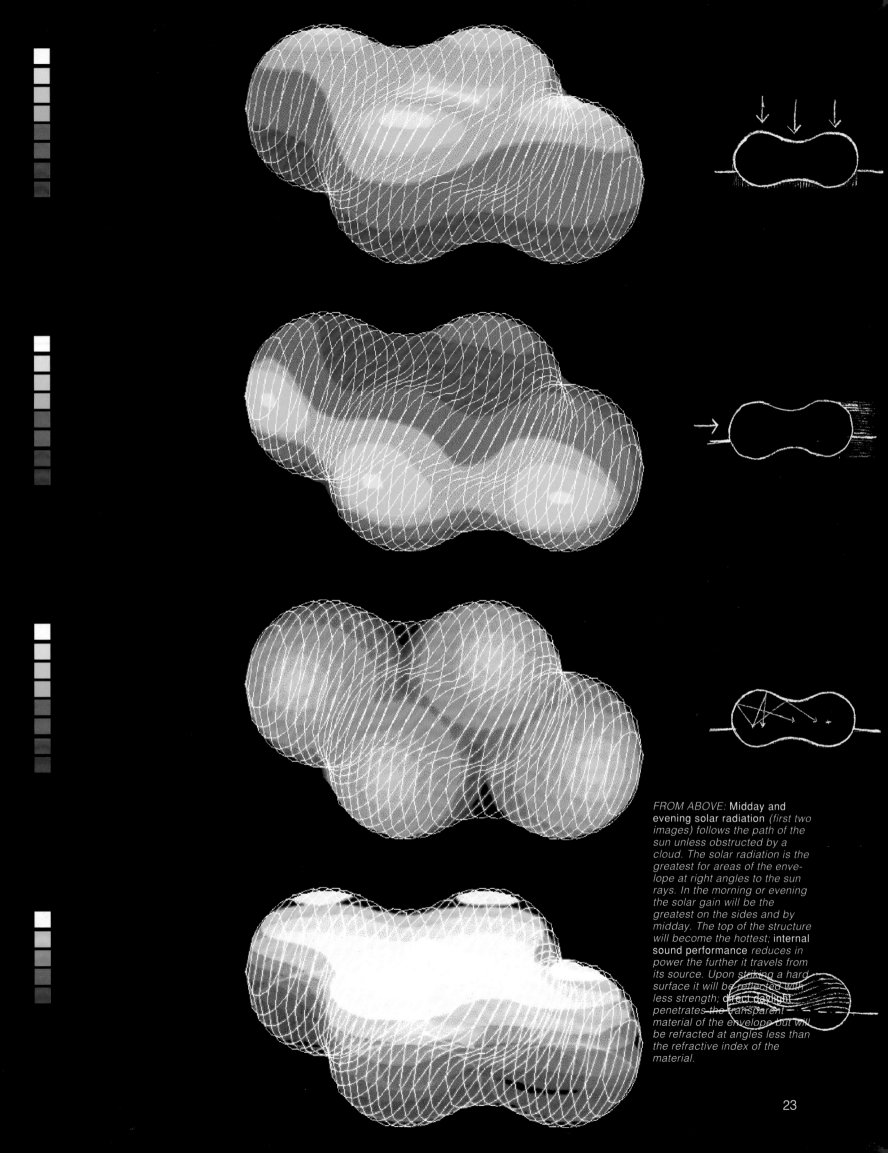

FROM ABOVE: **Midday and evening solar radiation** *(first two images) follows the path of the sun unless obstructed by a cloud. The solar radiation is the greatest for areas of the envelope at right angles to the sun rays. In the morning or evening the solar gain will be the greatest on the sides and by midday. The top of the structure will become the hottest;* **internal sound performance** *reduces in power the further it travels from its source. Upon striking a hard surface it will be reflected with less strength; direct daylight penetrates the transparent material of the envelope but will be refracted at angles less than the refractive index of the material.*

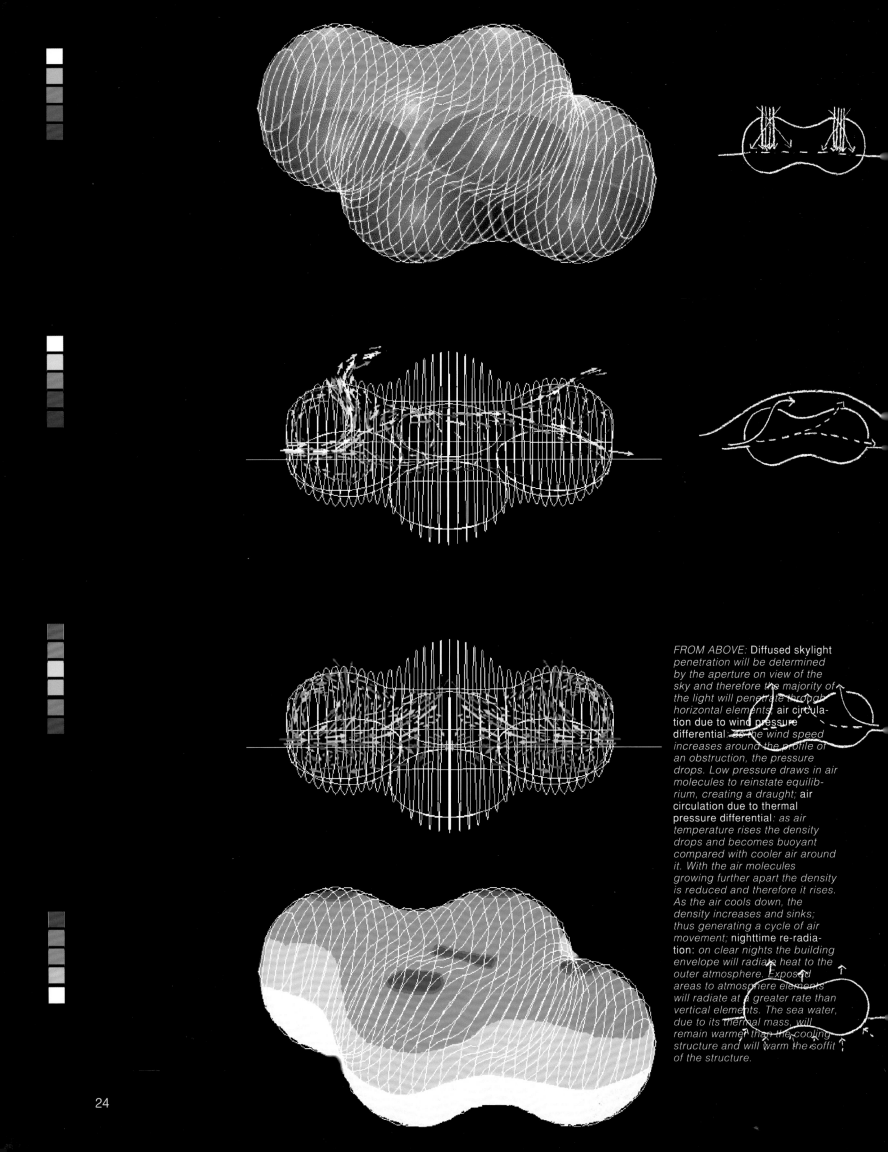

FROM ABOVE: Diffused skylight penetration will be determined by the aperture on view of the sky and therefore the majority of the light will penetrate through horizontal elements; air circulation due to wind pressure differential: as the wind speed increases around the profile of an obstruction, the pressure drops. Low pressure draws in air molecules to reinstate equilibrium, creating a draught; air circulation due to thermal pressure differential: as air temperature rises the density drops and becomes buoyant compared with cooler air around it. With the air molecules growing further apart the density is reduced and therefore it rises. As the air cools down, the density increases and sinks; thus generating a cycle of air movement; nighttime re-radiation: on clear nights the building envelope will radiate heat to the outer atmosphere. Exposed areas to atmosphere elements will radiate at a greater rate than vertical elements. The sea water, due to its thermal mass, will remain warmer than the cooling structure and will warm the soffit of the structure.

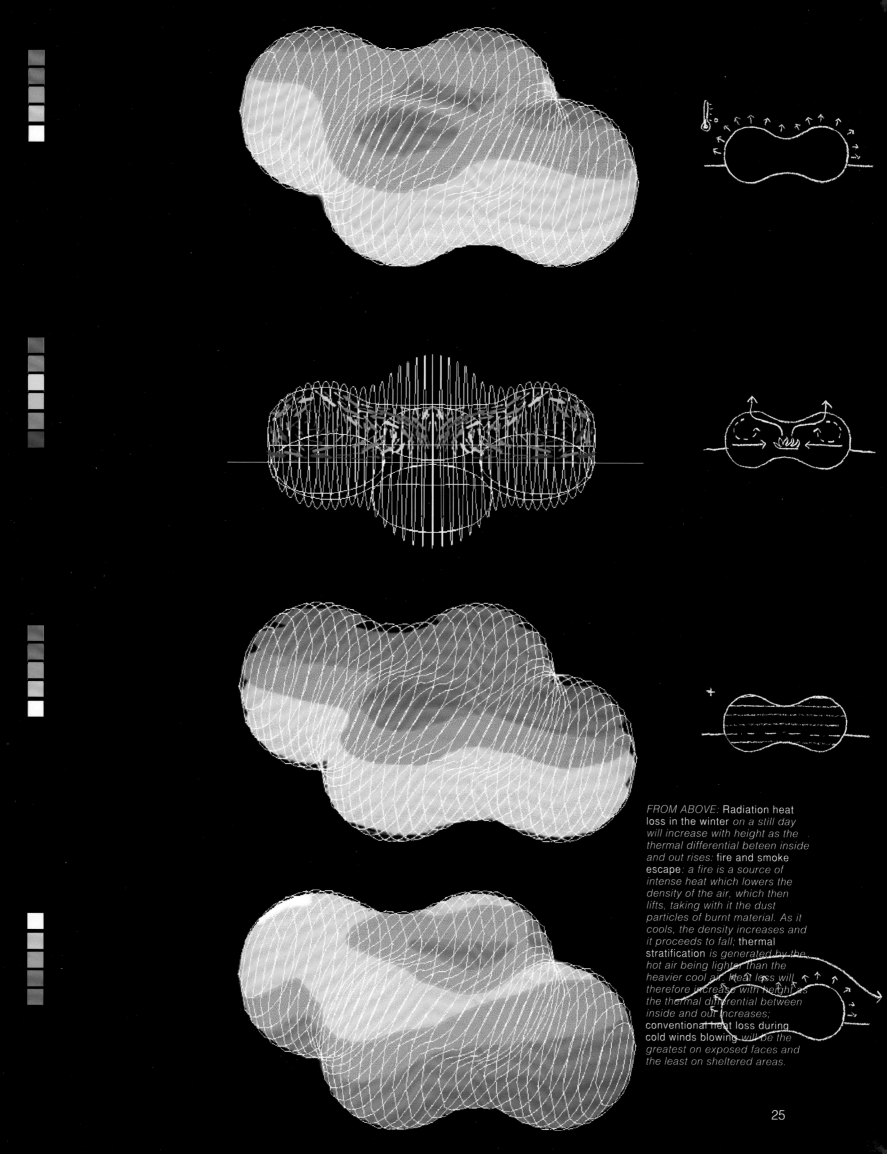

FROM ABOVE: Radiation heat loss in the winter *on a still day will increase with height as the thermal differential beteen inside and out rises:* fire and smoke escape: *a fire is a source of intense heat which lowers the density of the air, which then lifts, taking with it the dust particles of burnt material. As it cools, the density increases and it proceeds to fall;* thermal stratification *is generated by the hot air being lighter than the heavier cool air. Heat loss will therefore increase with height as the thermal differential between inside and out increases;* conventional heat loss during cold winds blowing *will be the greatest on exposed faces and the least on sheltered areas.*

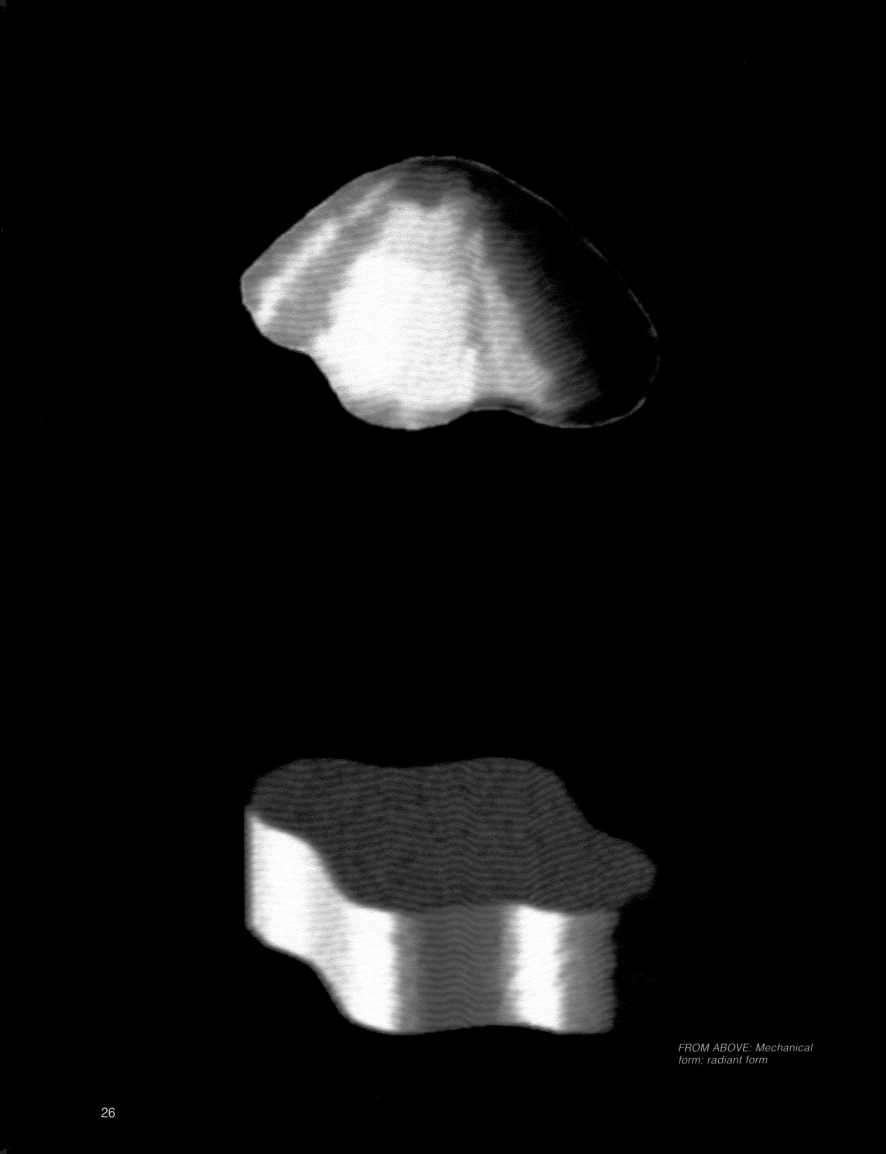

FROM ABOVE: Mechanical
form; radiant form

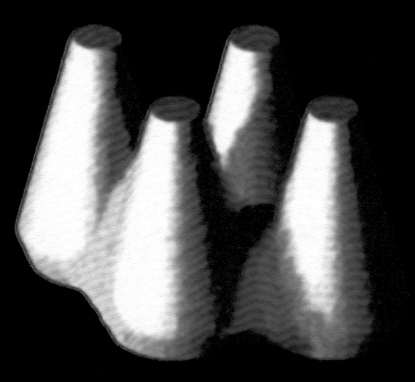

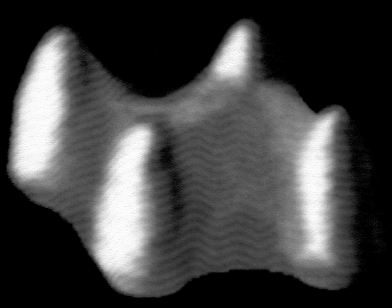

ATOMIC ARCHITECTURE

We presently process a variety of materials, cut them up into shapes and then fix them together to create the built environment for our particular needs. The majority of design resources are directed into trying to solve the technical problems brought about by the bringing together of different building components, whether they be structural, finishes, or service equipment of varying magnitude.

However, the advancement of material science is revealing a new construction process initiated at atomic level. Instead of cutting and stitching a patchwork of structural and non structural elements together in the hope that they will work in harmony, the atomic revolution will provide us with the means of creating building enclosures by the means of manipulating the molecular matrix and the atomic ingredients to the required structural and environmental specification, thus designing out the problem of building component interfaces. For example, using chemistry one will be able to orchestrate molecular geometry, transforming the material's strength and stiffness towards transparency without interruption. One can also even visualise the possibility of restructuring the very earth which bears the building to provide the necessary stiffness without the need for pouring thousands of tons of concrete into the ground in the form of foundations.

Molecular research into material performance is being approached by all building material and systems suppliers. In particular, the plastics industry and institutions including ICI and Cranfield University are investing huge resources into polymer research and development including being able to construct industrial components from small molecules without the necessity of melting and casting. The cloning of such a process will herald a new technical revolution in mass production of recycled atoms and molecular matrices.

This article focuses upon plastics technology. It examines the combination of carbon and hydrogen atoms and how they may be arranged in a variety of different geometrical configurations to create a range of different structural and environmental properties. It first briefly summarises the scope of plastics architecture and then describes in more detail the atomic structure of

carbon and hydrogen which are the chemical ingredients of most plastics. It is completed with a brief insight into how polymer atomic science may construct strength, stiffness, transparency and insulation from different arrangements of carbon and hydrogen atoms.

Plastic Architecture

The architectural characteristics of plastics are more commonly associated with their manufacturing processes than with the properties of molecular configuration of the material. There are four main types of manufacture:

– injection moulded elements   – spouts
– cast/extruded elements   – pipes
– woven fibres   – tents
– reinforced resins   – yachts

There are over 10,000 different types of plastics which may be soft, tough, hard, brittle, transparent, opaque, combustible, self-extinguishing or incombustible and insulative or conductive. Plastics are organic materials based on carbon and hydrogen atoms. They are polymers, consisting of relatively simple repeating units combined into very large chains. They are called plastics because at some stage they are plastic; that is they can be formed into desired shapes in the liquid state, often by pressure and heat.

Our construction industry has evolved from the stone age into the iron age and now is a leading consumer into the plastics age. Presently, the world production of plastics outstrips production of steel and aluminium together and is expected to nearly double in the next twenty years. Our industry is the second major consumer of plastics after the packaging industry, and it is used with applications ranging from drain pipes to resin coated fabric roofs enclosing our stadia.

Molecular Structure of Plastics

The understanding of the molecular structure of common plastics starts with the carbon and hydrogen atoms and then follows with an examination of the different arrangements the carbon and hydrogen atoms may take up to become 'plastic' molecules.

Carbon atoms
The carbon atom is not solid. It consists of a

OPPOSITE: How atoms react with themselves or other atoms to create molecules of totally different characteristics is under investigation throughout the world; FROM ABOVE: A 1900 Thatcher using a leggatt to beat the thatch firmly into position; 19th-century molecular model of Mono-chloromethane; JJ Thomson (1856-1940) intended to be a railway engineer, but instead became a brilliant physicist. He discovered the atomic structure of atoms by passing cathode rays between high voltage terminals in a glass filled with low pressure gas

nucleus around which electrons orbit. If the atom was the size of Wembley Stadium the nucleus would be smaller than a tennis ball. The nucleus consists of protons and neutrons which are about 10^{-15} m across and have a mass of 1.7 x 10^{-27} kg. The electrons which orbit the nucleus are about one 2000th of the mass of a proton. The electrons are held in orbit by an electrical force similar to that of the static force one experiences when one combs one's dry hair. Carbon atoms are living atmospheres of energy, mostly empty space dotted with particles.

If the force between the atomic particles is broken, huge amounts of energy are released. A process more commonly associated with nuclear explosions and nuclear reactors. The width of a razor blade is over one billion atoms wide. However atoms can be visualised. Some of the best images have been generated by scanning the electrical variations related to the positions of the atoms with a scanning tunnel microscope. By recording these variations, the position of atoms may be determined.

Hydrogen atom

The hydrogen atom is much smaller than the carbon atom as it only consists of a single proton and an electron in orbit. Hydrogen is the smallest atom on earth.

Plastic Molecule

When two or more atoms come into contact, they may have no effect or they may react to form a new molecule. This is a chemical reaction. The carbon atom requires four additional electrons in its outer orbit to become stable. The hydrogen atom requires one more electron in its single orbit to become stable. Atoms are able to share electrons with other atoms to become stable, for example a single carbon atom may share four electrons with four neighbouring carbon atoms in a number of configurations:

– Tetrahedron   – Diamond
– Plane   – Graphite
– Sphere   – Buckminsterfullerene

Two hydrogen atoms may share electrons to form ordinary hydrogen gas, annotated as H_2.

In addition, the carbon atom may share the electrons with four hydrogen atoms creating CH_4 methane gas. However, adjacent carbon atoms can share electrons as well as sharing electrons with hydrogen atoms, creating C_2H_4 or ethylene.

Ethylene is the start of the carbon-hydrogen chain. Ethylene molecules may be activated to form a much longer chain. The chain starts as a monomer, then a dimmer, then a trimmer and so on to become chains of hundreds containing thousands of carbon and hydrogen atoms commonly known as polymers.

A chain based on ethylene C_2H_4 is called polyethylene, a well-known plastic, providing for example vapour barrier films and water pipes.

Atomic Structural and Environmental Engineering

Atomic structural and environmental engineering in architecture is concerned with maximising the use of atoms in configurations for the physical and environmental benefit of the user. Building structures require four fundamental performances including: support, light control, thermal control and ventilation.

There are perhaps fifty different types of atoms which may be orchestrated into geometries which fulfil each or a combination of the above needs. However, this article limits the discussion to the design developments of the carbon and hydrogen atoms only, as a simple means of demonstrating how one may design and manipulate the atomic structure for particular structural and environmental requirements, a process now known as Nano Technology.

Nano Techology

Scientists are daily creating new material properties by changing the atomic or molecular configuration. There are over a ninety different types of atoms and there is an infinite number of possible arrangements from which molecules may be formed. This indeed means that any desired mechanical or environmental property may be acquired upon demand. In fact, the scientists who place atoms on top of atoms in a similar manner to carrying and laying bricks on a building site call their operation architecture.

For example, carbon atoms may be rearranged from their weaker graphite formation into the strong diamond formation by pressurising the graphite layers together until they interlock to form the diamond tetrahedron geometry. In 1990, the Buckminster Fuller geodesic dome principle was reconstructed in carbon atoms, creating a single 'Buckminsterfullerene' molecular ball of 60 carbon atoms which forms an ideal lubricant.

Atomic architects are making huge strides in the creation of new molecules which have never existed before. Computers are used, very much in the way we simulate building form, to help the atomic designer to test various atomic arrangements before proceeding with construction. Construction may consist of exerting pressures or may be more sophisticated by using construction tools such as processors which harvest particular atoms for treatment. These processors themselves consist of 'constructed' synthetic molecules. Beyond building matter the 'atomic designers' are developing synthetic drugs which are designed to seek out and destroy diseases as well as replacing damaged organisms.

FROM ABOVE: Atoms are mostly empty space with tiny sub-atomic particles suspended in a cloud of energy. Charged with static electrical effects, like the electrical atomosphere in a thunder storm; scanning tunnelling microscope image which shows a single layer of carbon atoms in the form of graphite; OPPOSITE, FROM ABOVE L TO R: Bird's eye view of Hampton Court by Leonard Knyss in the early 18th century; newly created market such as windsurfing generates opportunities which can trigger research, just as a new product of the plastic age can create a new market; molecules are made with atoms. They become bonded together like human links on a free fall; atomic engineers use computer programs to construct molecules. The atoms are colour coded and positioned. Their positions can be modified and new atoms or groups of atoms can be added. The computer stores information about the forces between these atoms

Atomic Architecture

Fundamental structural and environmental performance requirements may be created through the selection of suitable atoms arranged in an appropriate manner.

Atomic construction

There are four fundamental structural/environmental material properties required:-
- strength
- stiffness
- insulation
- transparency

The following section describes how each of these properties may be achieved by rearranging the carbon and hydrogen atomic framework.

Strength

Unbranched carbon-hydrogen chains are denser and stronger than the more 'jumbled' configuration of branched chains, thus like pruning a rose tree the configuration may be pruned to become more linear. Cross-linking of the chains also increases the strength. The cross-linking of chains transforms a collection of individual atomic chains to a single solid molecule which is the basis of setting resins used in GRP boat construction.

The strength of polyethylenes may be transformed by replacing the hydrogen atom with another. If the hydrogen atoms are replaced with Fluorine for example, it then becomes a polymer known as POLYTETRAFLUORO-ETHYLENE, more commonly known as PTFE which is the resin used for most high strength tensile fabric roofs.

Stiffness

Stiffness is the ratio of the force of deformation. In polyethylene the carbon to carbon is stronger than carbon to hydrogen bond. Thus eliminating a pair of hydrogen atoms and doubling up the carbon to carbon bond of adjacent carbon atoms will increase the stiffness. Stiffness of the material may also be increased by 'straightening up' the molecular chain from a jumble to a more rational linear form.

If a cubic molecular structure is generated (as for rubber) the molecules may be elongated, and with the necessary applied energy, such as heat, the atoms will return to their original atomic configuration. These atomic frames are more commonly known as shape memory materials. If you heat an elastic band under tension for example, it will become shorter.

In the aerospace industry, vast resources are being invested into the research associated with the deformation and re-establishment of carbon-hydrogen geometry, to eliminate inflight thermal deformation of the plastic structural components of the wings and fuselage.

The deformation is counteracted by the atoms repeatedly returning to their original position. If such principles were developed for building components, one could imagine infinite stiffness for very little material, creating a new age in elegant structural design.

Insulation

As the temperature of a material rises, the atoms vibrate. The closer the atoms are to each other, the quicker the heat is transmitted. In gases for example, the atoms/molecules are further apart. This is why practical insulating materials are those that can successfully contain gas volumes above 90%. This may be achieved by raising the temperature of a polymer above the melting point where the inter-molecular forces holding the long chain molecules are broken down. Also the intermolecular forces that maintain a rigid linear configuration break down and the molecules coil up with each other in a manner analogous with boiling spaghetti on cooling. If on cooling, the atomic designer was able to maintain a vacuum between molecular chains, one would be able to generate super insulating properties, far in excess of what is presently available, ie a material as thin as this paper having insulative properties equivalent to over a foot of concrete.

Transparency

If the wavelength of light is able to pass through the molecular configuration, the material is known as transparent.

To ensure the polymer is transparent, the atomic designer needs to disrupt the packing efficiency of the polymer chains by rearranging the carbon-hydrogen molecular configuration to allow the free passage of light rays.

Conclusion

Thus provided with the knowledge and the 3D computer modelling facilities already available in most architectural and engineering offices, an architect too may proceed to generate a new understanding of materials at an atomic level with which we have all become so familiar.

Imagine designing an atomic structure, for example, which absorbed water molecules from a humid atmosphere and transmits them to the outside to be evaporated by solar radiation. Such a roofing and cladding material would provide humidity control for large public spaces in the tropics, thus avoiding the huge energy demand being sought by air conditioned airport terminals in the Far-East.

It is strange to think that if one replaced the carbon atom with a silicon atom and pairs of hydrogen atoms with oxygen, one would create from the common polythene chain the molecular basis for glass. Atomic architecture is more to

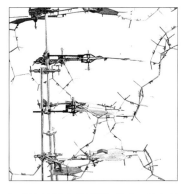

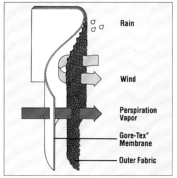

FROM ABOVE: In 1953 James Watson and Francis Crick made the DNA model. It comprises a large number of repeated elements with aluminium plates representing the four different bases; gortex material allows for the passage of air molecules but restrains water molecules

do with experiencing the mystery of 'atomic space planning' than solving the technical problems generated by the interaction of inappropriate materials. It may not be in our life time, although many scientists believe it will be when architects and engineers may design and construct a building from common atoms such as carbon, hydrogen, oxygen, silica, calcium and iron. In the future, the design team will be able to create the environmental space from a coherent arrangement of atoms which provide the necessary passive and active interaction with gravity, air movement and radiation for the least amount of atoms. These building materials may even be self-repairing. The high technology, not of the future but of the present.

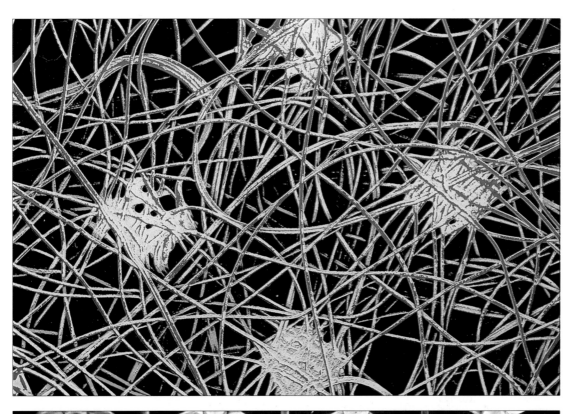

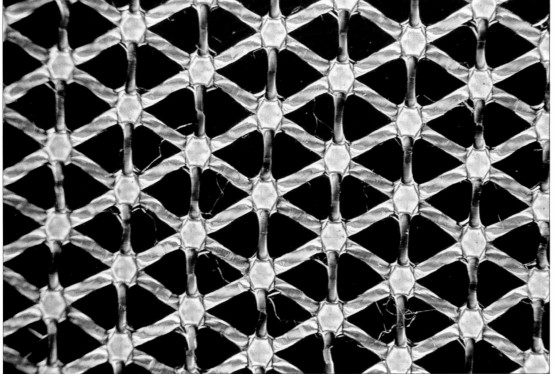

FROM ABOVE: False colour scanning electron micrograph (SEM) of the detailed structure of polypropylene (or polypropene) filaments. The filaments of this non-woven textile fabric are anchored by heat bonding. RE Litchfield; polarised light micrograph of a section of a biaxially oriented, stretched, high-density polythene net. This fabric is machined from man-made polythene fibres. The colours in the fibres appear in polarised light and correspond to residual stresses in the plastic fibres. Dr Harold Rose.

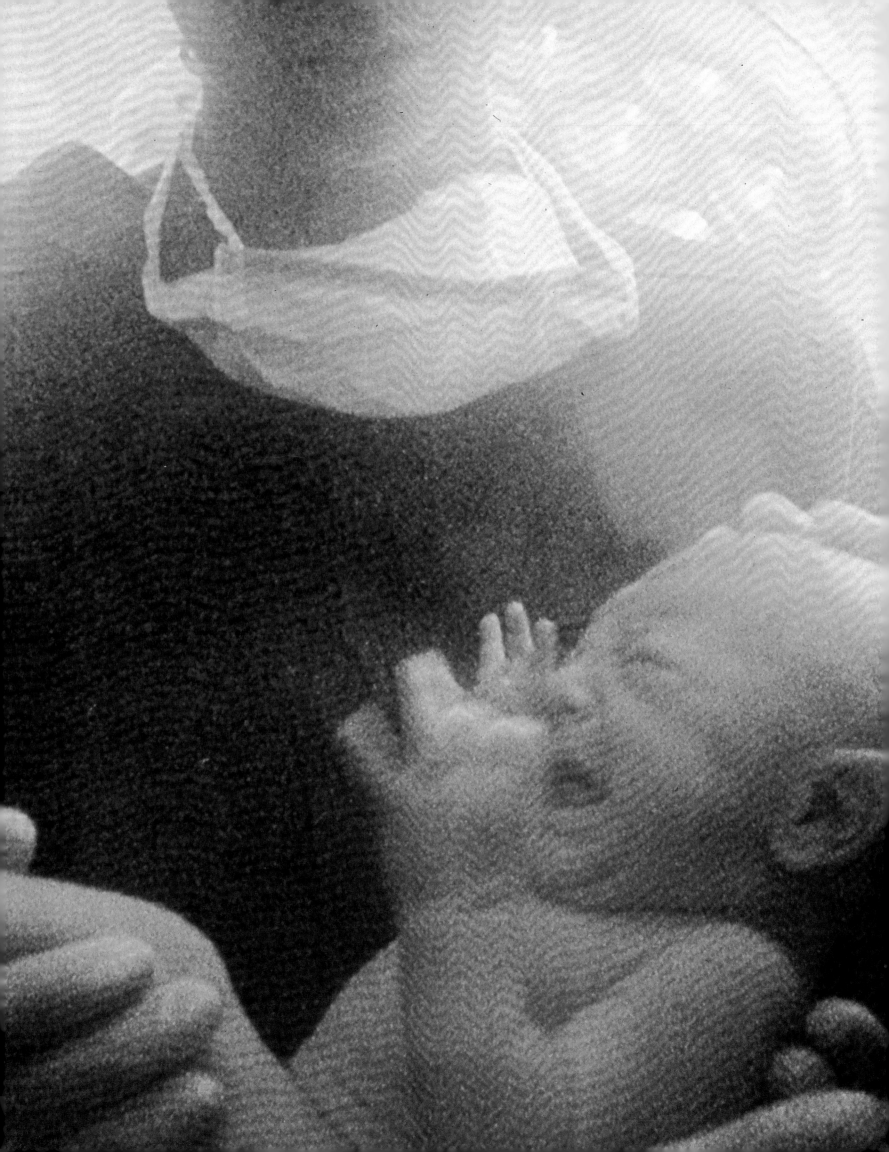

THE POWER OF THE BRIEF

The primary goal of engineering is to maximise the use of materials, energy and skills for the benefit of mankind.

Before an engineer may proceed to collaborate with architects in engineering a building or new town it is imperative know what the architect is trying to achieve. Then a discussion may be initiated on how such a vision may be best engineered with available resources.

Too often, designers launch into the design process to achieve an architectural statement without the necessary research and analysis of all the issues associated with the creation of a quality brief. In particular, the brief for the internal and micro-climatic environment should consider appropriate definition of the parameters of light, sound, temperature, and air movement.

Presently, comfort is associated with extreme environmental control in terms of fixing the quantity of ventilation, humidity, light, heat and cooling to precise levels. The ultimate in comfort has been described by property agents as the tightest control which may only be achieved by sealing the building and servicing it with conditioned air. However, providing such tight control requires the installation of expensive air conditioning equipment which results in high energy demands upon our limited resources.

We are beginning to understand that the environmental brief requires much more than specification of universal rates which have little to do with the particular needs of the users or the climatic context. Our understanding of perception and comfort is lacking but we are starting to realise the complexity and unpredictablity involved; as varied as are individuals and climatic zones.

What is clear is that the old idea of a homogeneously maintained environment is being seriously challenged. To the new generation of architects and engineers, the old specification for working environments – 500 lux across the working plane, air at a constant temperature of 21°C and four air changes per hour – is anathema.

This is a response to long-unheard building users, whose views are at last being sought in a market-oriented age. In a recent survey carried out for property consultants Richard Ellis, Harris Research interviewed 480 directors and senior managers. Ninety per cent of them said they preferred a building without air conditioning, many believing that natural daylighting and effective ventilation are important design features. Air conditioning was so unpopular, in fact, that financial institutions with investments in air conditioned buildings should be seriously concerned. Why invest in costly air conditioned developments which are less valuable to the user than low cost passive engineering solutions?

This survey indicates that for the first time this century our industry is in a demand-led market. But our attempts to understand this deep and unknown realm are still in their early stages. Current methods include quantifying temperature comfort by smelling armpits to classify BO, and charting space according to the percentage of people dissatisfied (PPD). However there are new tools emerging – based on the use of computers to model the environment in three dimensions – which enable the beginning of a description of the variety and interaction between elements. The task is not to define all-inclusive solutions, for we know that this is impossible, but to explore the mystery of the interaction of natural forces. We may then be able to create spaces providing the variety of conditions that human experience demands.

Climatic Awareness

The human body is extremely sensitive to variations in light, heat, sound, touch and airborne smells, but perception varies dramatically from person to person. People will not agree unanimously on their preferred climatic condition, especially if they are foreign in a particular climate.

In northern countries, people prefer to walk on the sunny side of the street whereas southern Europeans prefer to walk on the shaded side. Religions of the Northern hemisphere are based upon the solar cycle whereas those nearer the Equator are based upon the lunar cycle. Mistral winds in southern France are not considered a problem by the locals who accept their coming as natural – as the rise and fall of the tides.

How different are the characters of the seafarer and his opposite, the inland farmer. One so responsive to challenge and eager in its pursuit,

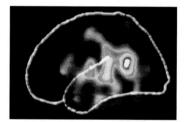

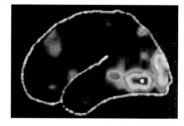

OPPOSITE: The moment of birth into our artificial environment. Photograph Pictor International; FROM ABOVE: The mystery of human behaviour; Positron Electron Tomography scan images of the brain for hearing and seeing

and the other cast in tradition and resistant to change. The different environments have created different characteristics, the different individuals dwell in different worlds.

There is no doubt that unpredictable climate makes nations more inventive in unpredictable weather. The experience of planning a barbecue at the weekend, to be spoilt by rain falling as our guests arrive makes us responsive to disappointment and induces us to seek an alternative. Does a more tempered climate influence a nation of tolerance, and a more stable and predictable climate influence a nation into becoming more organised? People living in extreme climates are focused on survival, but those in kinder climates are more at ease with the climate.

Perception also changes over time. During the summer, northern Europeans migrate to southern Europe's hotter climate in search of a more reliable sun to create their image-conscious tan, but in the last century tanning of the skin was avoided by the upper classes who associated it with labourers of the field. Nowadays weekend visitors pay a premium for views of the countryside whereupon local farmers construct buildings which look inwards, preferring to forget the outside once within. In the last century railway passengers would draw their curtains while travelling through the Alps, to avoid looking at the rocky wilderness. Now we pay a premium for views from ski chalets, and wilderness is our ultimate idea of beauty.

In buildings, we know that perception of comfort is directly related to the form and environment of the building. For example people in sealed air conditioned buildings are sensitive to minor variations in temperature and light level – leaving them very vulnerable to air conditioning system underperformance or breakdown (a major contributory factor to the association between air conditioning and sick building syndrome). But in buildings where people can open the window and experience the external climate conditions, their expectations become adjusted to the seasons, and their tolerance of variation increases dramatically. It is also clear that the influence on comfort of radiant, as opposed to convective, heat is often underestimated.

Building users' perception of the environment and climate is complex and diverse, everchanging with historical tradition, geographical location and between individuals. These variations cannot be standardised simply to make the life of property agents easier. The challenge is to give engineering and architectural interpretation to this variety.

The Art of Environmental Engineering

Environmental design is the science and art of designing and making large enclosures and building units with economy and creativity, so that they can respond to climatic forces to which they may be subjected. Our industry needs to expand upon environmental engineering practice, design development and research, education and training in association with artists of all disciplines.

How can we be creative about light, temperature, air movement and sound? More generally, how does the sense of 'naturalness', or contact with the outdoors affect people's acceptance of a varying internal environment. With the development of intelligent buildings and increasing internal climate control, how is user-control to be integrated with automatic control? There are also issues of the 'politics' of workplace control – who opens windows or regulates solar penetration, light and ventilation? What balance should there be between user comfort and management stimulation? Is there a natural aesthetic link between building form and its response to the climate and how may the designers make their operations more 'legible' to the user?

There are many more questions than answers and we must look for new relationships with art. Perhaps a greater role for artists in building design should be created in the development of the environmental brief – rather than their staid role in adding objects of art to the built form?

Architecture embraces many arenas including the art of performance. Education in our schools, including painting, sculpture, drawing and music, is fundamental training for individuals to assist the growth of their awareness of natural forces, and of how those forces may be coherently balanced within a single constructed form.

The art of environmental design is a growing market with a premium. It will not be too long before we see the rents for buildings of environmental quality and variety outstrip that of air conditioned ones. Architects need to take the lead and utilise their communications skills to inform property investors of the potentially rich returns for context-sensitive environmental design – and of the risks associated with homogenous values for comfort conditions. Our problem is that we have become so involved in product design that we are more interested in what we can build, instead of why.

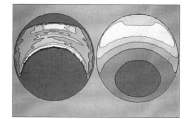

OPPOSITE: On rabante la grande-voile, par gros-temps, a bord du *Garthsnaid (photomontage)*; *FROM ABOVE: The eyes of the female housefly are made up of 4,000 ommatidia, each of which sees a fragment of the world; computer modelling of daylight dispersion; measurement of the unit of smell – the Olf*

FLUX – DESIGN FOR CHANGE

The new headquarters for the telecommunications company Ionica at Cambridge forms a practical demonstration of the principles of environmental design for an ever-changing variety of human comfort expectations. Designed in close cooperation between the client, the engineers and the architect, it set out to allow variation in conditions over the day and the year while remaining within certain fixed limits. The principle is one of environmental control by structure, where the form and fabric of the building are used to manipulate the changes in prevailing conditions to create a comfortable and dynamic interior.

Cedric Price recently urged architects to become more cognisant of time – undoubtedly the quintessential modern dimension. Buckminster Fuller observed that pollution is merely a resource in the wrong place, and we are beginning to realise that a demand for heating or cooling is merely energy available *at the wrong time*.

The advent of complex but affordable iterative calculation has enabled us to translate this insight into building form. In the old days of glass curtain-walled buildings with giant air conditioning plant, engineers merely executed the calculations that were possible within their limited resources of time and calculating power – carrying out a clerical exercise to determine the size of plant necessary to cope with peak conditions in such a building. The resulting plant was oversized for most conditions and wasteful of energy; however, a static calculation was not expected to be accurate for more than a few moments of time.

The dynamic calculations now available through computers enable buildings to be designed for many different moments of time – when used to provide a useful description of behaviour on the right scale of operation (as opposed to the macro-scale of weather patterns and the micro-scale of molecular behaviour). The Ionica building is designed on the basis of a detailed understanding of how its components interact with the climate and occupants from day to day and season to season, based on complex computer analysis.

The challenge is to respond to a typical Cambridge year of weather, passing through a cycle of old winter, warm mid-season and hot summer. To ensure that the occupants do not become too warm in the summer and too cool in the winter, the structure, materials and form are used as a climatic modulator, though the principles of operation vary for each season – the main images opposite describe the principles of operation for the day and night condition in each season. The principal elements consist of ventilated standard precast hollow-core slabs, adjustable facades with shading, a central atrium and wind towers. The whole is controlled by a Building Energy Management System (BEMS) which constantly monitors internal and external conditions, opening and closing windows and wind tower vents, adjusting the background lighting level, opening windows and operating fans where necessary. Occupants also have full local control enabling them to vary conditions at will.

The building layout consists of two daylit linear blocks oriented on an east-west axis. Cores are located at the east and west ends to block out low angle sun and overhangs provided on the southern facade control high angle summer sun while allowing for solar gain from low-angle winter sun.

During the mid-season period the building is naturally ventilated. The wind towers in combination with the thermal stack effect in the atria create cross-ventilation for the offices. In the winter, heat loss is minimised and solar gain is maximised. The heat from the top of the atria is used to preheat fresh air ducted to the offices. During the summer the cool night air is vented through the hollow core slabs so they perform as 'chilled' slabs during the heat of the day. In peak summer periods, for what is expected to be one per cent of the time, precooled air is supplied to the offices at low level where most beneficial.

Floors are precast hollow core slabs, which act as heat stores; in summer absorbing the heat of day to reject it at night, and in winter preserving the relative warmth of day against the night's cold. The atrium of the building can itself catch heat when required and uses wind and stack effects for cross-ventilation of the building in summer, bringing cooling air movement across the occupants.

The process is difficult to visualise in static images. Opposite, in the background, are stills from a computer animation created to describe the operation of the building over a day and night in early or late summer, and which proves strangely hypnotic viewing even though it is soundless; captivating and subverting normal perception like time-lapse photography of changing weather patterns. It shows the air flows through the building created by stack effect and wind suction; and the change in slab temperature through the day and night. During the day, the slab is cooler than the air, and its exposed soffit radiates coolness to the building occupants. Towards the end of the day, the slab heats up, reaching its maximum temperature in the early evening when the building's occupiers have gone home. At night, air is blown through the hollow cores absorbing heat, precooling the slab for the next summer day to come.

Ionica was designed as a moving picture, not a still. Nevertheless, it is interesting that some of its most prominent architectural features are those concerned with environmental control by structure; the wind towers, the shading devices, and form of the building itself. It is the beginning of an architecture which has thrown off stylistic preferences to create form through complex dynamic function.

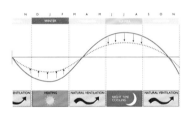

FROM ABOVE: Elevation; view of southern window with solar shading; internal view. Photographs Timothy Soar; principle of seasonal operation showing 'peak-lopping' of the energy demand curve'; OPPOSITE: Diagrams of seasonal operation conditions of the building, over stills from a computer animation created by Mark Wise

Architect: RH Partnership, Cambridge
Environmental Control by Structure Consultants: Battle McCarthy
Service Engineers: Rybka Smith Ginsler & Battle
Structural Engineers: Hannah Reed Associates
Quantity Surveyor: Davis Langdon & Everest
Draughting & Acoustic Consultants: Cambridge Architectural Research
Wind Tunnel Studies: Bristol Aeronautical Research

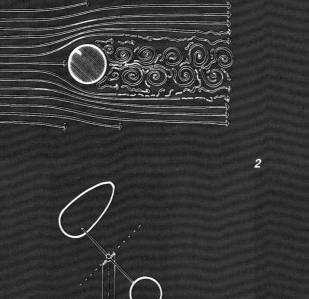

1 *Turbulent flow in the wake of a cylinder in water*

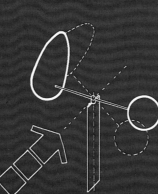

2 *Cigarette smoke moving from laminar to turbulent flow*

3 *Sphere and streamlined masses on a frictionless pivot. Note, both masses have the same maximum diameter*

4 *When a wind load is applied the sphere has a greater resistance. Streamlining reduces the resistance to air flow*

5 *Two spheres are placed on a frictionless pivot. One has a smooth surface, the other is roughened*

6 *When a high velocity wind load is applied the smooth sphere has a greater resistance. At high velocities the drag of the rough ball can be anything up to one fifth of the drag of the smooth ball, ie a dimpled golf ball can travel up to five times as far as a smooth golf ball*

7 *Aerofoil in laminar flow*

8 *When the aerofoil is turned it creates boundary layer separation and results in turbulent air patterns*

9 *Hang-glider – laminar flow across aerofoil wing generates lift.*

10 *A fish has a low drag shape to ease movement through water*

SHAPE, TEXTURE AND FLOW

Before Galileo performed his apocryphal experiment at the Leaning Tower of Pisa, the philosophers believed that feathers fell more slowly than metal balls because they weighed less. Now we know differently. They fall more slowly because the air resistance opposing the motion of the feathers is much greater than that on the metal balls.

The aim of this article is to present some insights concerning the flow of fluids around objects streamlined and non-streamlined, rough and smooth, through a series of experiments. Individually, those illustrated seem to fit no clear pattern of behaviour. We hope to explain how order may be brought out of what seems to be chaos through the grasp of a relatively small number of fundamental concepts and governing physical principles, in order to begin a discussion of the fundamentals of shape, texture and air flow for high-rise towers.

Wind

As warm air rises it is supplemented by fresh air being drawn in at low level. This drawing in of air is known as wind. Winds occur at a global scale, as trade or prevailing winds, and at a local scale, as off- and onshore winds.

Engineering wind for buildings

This evolved from the aeronautical industry. The wind tunnel used to develop Concorde has also been used since the sixties to investigate the performance of wind around existing structures, and as a design tool for new buildings and external spaces. But an essential understanding of wind effects is still lacking in a large part of the architectural and engineering community.

There are several basic principles of wind behaviour around buildings. When air molecules hit objects they apply a force to the object (the faster they are travelling, the greater the force). As they pass around an object, they accelerate to keep track with those in the main body of the flow, and the pressure drops. The molecules pass each other like a pack of cards slipping, known as a laminar flow.

In tall buildings, there are six principal areas of interest: wind effects around the base; lateral loads on structure; dynamic loads on structure; lateral loads on facade elements; wind ventilation; and wind power. As the wind strikes a tower it applies a force, which is opposed by the structural cores, while reducing the exposed area to prevailing winds may also reduce this force. Some air molecules will go around the tower, some will be deflected upwards or downwards. Those deflected upwards pass over the top; it is at this position that one would place a wind generator. Those cast downwards will hit the base of the tower and be deflected back into the path of the oncoming wind, resulting in unpredictable conditions for pedestrians at the base of the tower. To reduce this effect, the wind may be carried around the perimeter of the tower along a 'wind gutter'.

The wind passing around the tower generates a drag force which has to be opposed by the stability cores. Paradoxically, a rough surface will experience a lower drag force. Any form not 'streamlined' into the prevailing wind will generate turbulence in the wake, which in certain conditions will be uneven, resulting in alternate forces at each side of the tower pushing the tower back and forth. This could be counteracted by allowing wind to pass through the tower at specific sections or diverting air around it through a wind shield, releasing it at points to vary the pressure along the height of the tower. Finally, the wind creates an outbalance force to be restrained by the stability core, though the imbalance of pressures may be used to aid ventilation from one side of the tower to the other.

Design for wind

'Morphology is not only the study of material things and the forms of material things, but its dynamical aspects in terms of force, of the operation of energy.' (D'Arcy Thompson, *On Growth and Form*, 1942)

Design for wind will increasingly involve hybrid tools: from active building elements such as wind shields to the passive, such as wind gutters or ribbed facades. Forms will change with wind direction and speed – their facades will incorporate wind activated panels linked into a central processing unit with a parallel processing neural network which can instantaneously regulate wind pressures externally as well as internally depending upon wind speed and direction. Such a system may display a form of metabolic homeostasis known as artificial intelligence – dynamic synthesis of the static form.

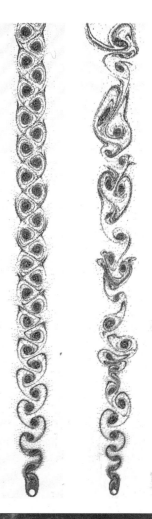

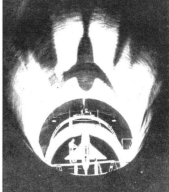

FROM ABOVE: Flow patterns of a cylinder through still water; flow patterns of a cylinder through turbulent water; wind tunnel testing of an aircraft fuselage

The authors would like to acknowledge the contribution made by Douglas Broadley, Robert Webb, Professor Graham of Imperial College and Dr Lawson of Bristol University Aeronautical Research.

GLOBAL WARNING

Thousands of satellites orbit the Earth, constantly monitoring scanning and photographing. The images and analyses that they have produced have shaped our perception of the earth – just as the first images of earth from space gave us the impression of a fragile and finite planet floating in an infinity of nothing, the satellite images paint an image of a dynamic and complex Earth, whose systems we are only just beginning to understand. These new eyes, combined with millions of measuring instruments on the surface of earth, have illustrated the environmental damage we are causing to the biosphere – they have shown us the ozone hole, and they record daily changes in the gaseous balance of the atmosphere, in global temperatures and in weather patterns.

The Earth Summit in Rio in June 1992 was the largest ever meeting of world leaders – over 100 of them came to pledge their countries to the principles and practice of sustainable development. The outcome was a series of international agreements – the Convention on Climate Change and the Convention on Biological Diversity included commitments to change, while the Forest Principles, the Rio Declaration and Agenda 21 were published as statements of intent. Most importantly, the Climate Treaty tied world governments to reducing carbon dioxide emissions to 1990 levels by 2000.

Little progress has been made since 1992. The follow-up to Rio held in Berlin in April 1995 found that many countries will fail to reach their commitments for the year 2000, while no further reductions have yet been agreed. The Berlin meeting also saw the fragmentation of global politics in a response to the nineties Zeitgeist – proceedings were dominated by two groups, the Alliance of Low-Lying Countries (including the Netherlands, Bangladesh and several island states) – who demanded reductions in CO_2 of 20 per cent by 2010 – and OPEC, the oil cartel which attempted to block all commitments to change.

There is controversy over the magnitude of global warming, but while scientists disagree on the exact predictions for change, the majority agree that change is inevitable on current trends. The International Energy Agency in Paris has predicted in March 1995 that to meet the needs of the developing world and to satisfy the increase in world population the annual energy consumption will increase by 30-40 per cent by the year 2010. Ninety per cent of this energy will be produced from fossil fuels, therefore the world CO_2 emissions are likely to increase by a similar percentage, which will result in global warming and rises in the sea level. Based upon historical data, the resultant temperature rise may be as much as 10^{0}C which would result in an increase of sea level of up to 1 metre. Climatic computer modelling being carried out in USA, UK and Germany predicts temperature rises of 12^{0}C, 8^{0}C and 4^{0}C respectively. Average temperatures have been rising steadily since 1860, but the predicted increases are on a completely different scale of change.

The increase of CO_2 in the atmosphere will generate global warming and, with the resultant sea level rises, will put billions of pounds worth of infrastructure and buildings worldwide under unacceptable risk of flooding, undermining commercial confidence in the heart of our coastal cities. The initial destructive force will be the devaluation of market values as properties become unacceptable investment risks in potential flood areas – not a case of returning home to find your property destroyed by a flood, but returning home to find that your home has become uninsurable and potentially worthless. Other destructive forces are only just beginning to be charted – for instance the growth of malaria. Sixty million square kilometres of the planet currently have the right conditions for malaria, which kills up to two million people a year. The change in global temperatures will increase malaria's range by 30 per cent, while doubling the area which is seasonally affected (in practice more dangerous, as epidemics are more likely in seasonally affected areas).

An editorial in *The Economist*, commenting on the Berlin meeting, recently claimed that 'environmentalists' efforts to scare the world over global warming seem not to have worked,' and argued for a do-nothing policy, as 'most actions would pose a bigger threat to human well-being than does global warming.'

Yet there is a raft of actions which will help

OPPOSITE: The largest structure ever to be moved on earth, being towed from its sheltered home in the Norwegian fjord of Yrkje, past Stavanger and out into the rough waters of the North Sea – the drilling platform Troll is 472 metres high, and weighs more than a million tonnes. It is 41 metres higher than the Empire State Building in New York ABOVE: wreck of the three-master Mildred on Gurnard's Head, 6 April, 1912; Robert Webb's proposal for a Millennium Forest on marginal land around the M25, generating electricity and heat for London

Global Warning

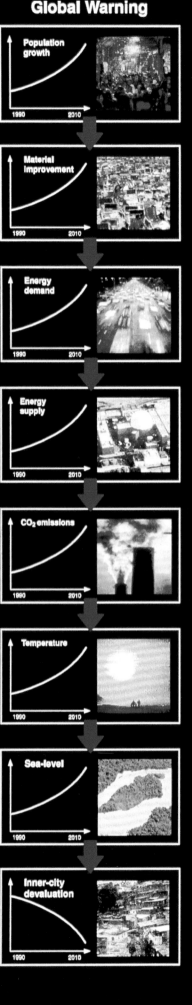

- Population growth
  1990 — 2010
- Material improvement
  1990 — 2010
- Energy demand
  1990 — 2010
- Energy supply
  1990 — 2010
- CO_2 emissions
  1990 — 2010
- Temperature
  1990 — 2010
- Sea-level
  1990 — 2010
- Inner-city devaluation
  1990 — 2010

Changes in Global Mean Sea Level and Average Surface Temperatures

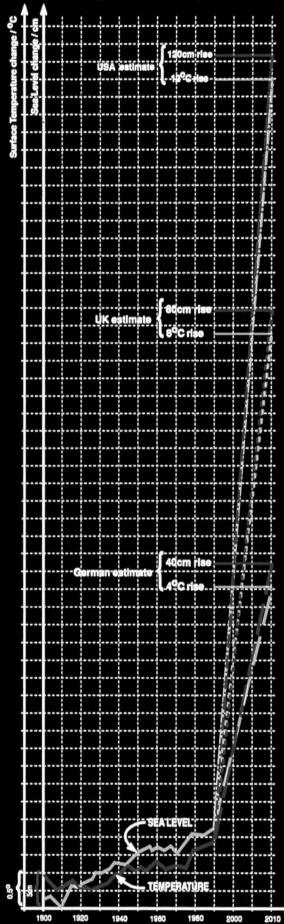

Surface Temperature change / °C

Sea Level change / cm

USA estimate { 120cm rise
               12°C rise }

UK estimate { 80cm rise
              8°C rise }

German estimate { 40cm rise
                  4°C rise }

SEA LEVEL

TEMPERATURE

0.5°   5cm

1900   1920   1940   1960   1980   2000   2010

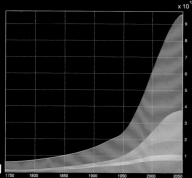

1 Asia | Africa | South America | North America | Europe
World population

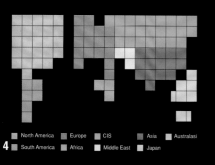

2

3

4 North America | Europe | CIS | Asia | Australasi
South America | Africa | Middle East | Japan

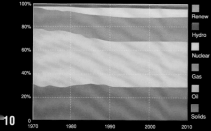

5 Per capita income by region in purchasing power parities
OECD | East Asia | FSU/CEE | China | Rest of World

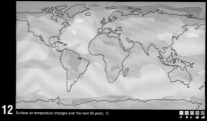

6 World energy consumption
Renew | Hydro | Nuclear | Gas | Oil | Solids
MTOE

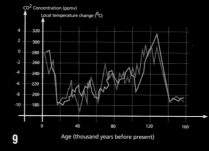

7 1990 | 2000 | 2010
OECD | FSU/CEF | ROW | TOTAL
Growth in Carbon Dioxide Emissions

8 Carbon dioxide emissions per terawatt hour of electricity
CEE | China | South Asia | Africa | East Asia | OECD | South & Central America

9 CO_2 Concentration (ppmv)
Local temperature change (^{0}C)
Age (thousand years before present)

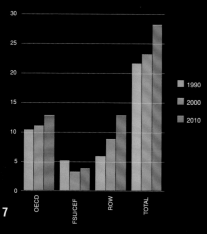

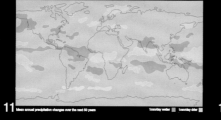

10 Renew | Hydro | Nuclear | Gas | Oil | Solids
World share of energy sources

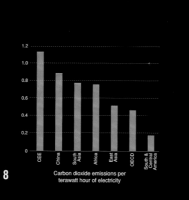

11 Mean annual precipitation changes over the next 50 years
1mm/day wetter | 1mm/day drier

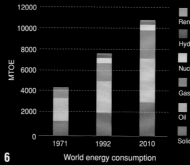

12 Surface air temperature changes over the next 50 years, °C

13 SOLAR (SHORT WAVE) RADIATION.
ATMOSPHERE
THERMAL (LONG WAVE) RADIATION.
EARTH

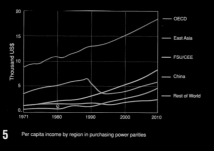

14

15

OPPOSITE: Global Warning: the cycle of change which leads to global warming and city devaluation; LEFT: World population has been growing since 1750, and is expected to reach 10 billion by 2050 (1). By 2000, a majority of the world population will live in cities (2, 3). Global energy consumption is currently highly inequitable (4), but with the continuing increase in world population (5), energy consumption will rise by 30% by 2010 (6). Carbon dioxide emissions will rise by a similar amount (7), though some parts of the world produce energy less efficiently than others (8). Predictions of global warming are based on historical evidence showing a close correlation between carbon dioxide concentration and local temperature (9). If present trends continue, most of the energy required will be generated from fossil fuel sources (10), and the global climate will alter in terms of temperature (11) and rainfall (12). Global warming is caused by the greenhouse effect, principally caused by carbon dioxide (13). The large-scale implementation of fuel crops like willow coppice on agricultural and marginal land across the world could reduce carbon dioxide emissions and prevent global warming (14, 15)

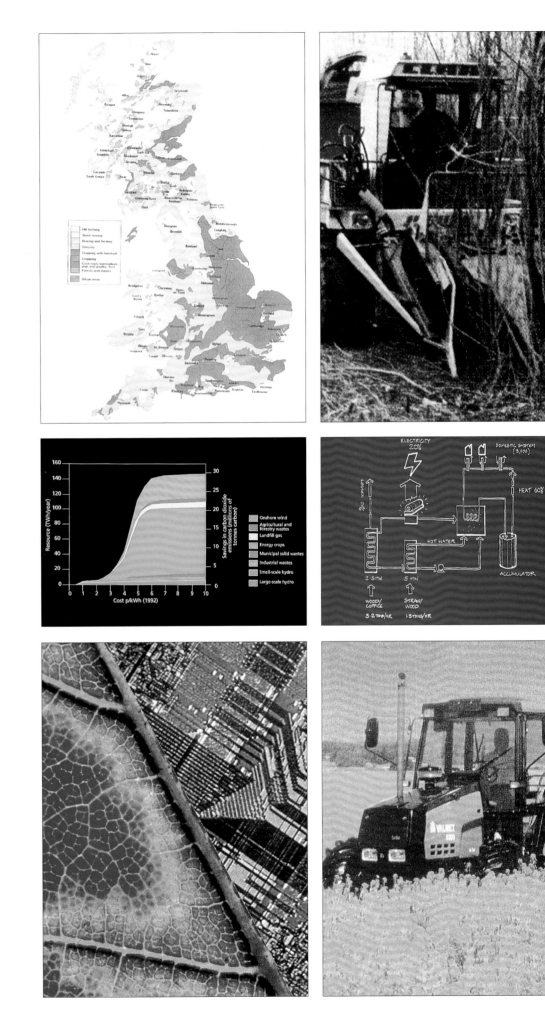

FROM ABOVE L TO R: Graph showing the potential renewable energy resource in the UK at a cost up to 10p/kWh (current electricity price is 7.5p/kWh) – the majority of the resource is represented by energy crops; map of the UK showing current agricultural uses; CLAAS forage harvester cutting willow coppice with a special cutting head – the wood is cut and chipped in one operation; schematic of a CHP system fired by straw (an agricultural waste material) and coppice (purpose-grown); the integration of nature and technology will lead to further efficiency; harvesting machinery can be fuelled on biodiesel produced from rape seed

to reduce carbon dioxide emissions while also stimulating economies and creating other benefits – measures which are 'win-win' in the language of *The Economist*. The policy of doing nothing at best achieves nothing, and at worst allows global warming to run rampant. Why pilot the aeroplane without controls, when the controls are laid out before us? What is required is large scale engineering – rigorous analysis which considers population, energy use, and carbon dioxide in the context of global energy production.

An example of such successful engineering is the introduction of sugar-cane alcohol as vehicle fuel in Brazil. Started in the late 1970s, this programme was so successful that in 1983, over 90 per cent of all new cars were alcohol fuelled, with alcohol providing about 20 per cent of Brazilian transportation fuels (originally stimulated by a mix of government subsidy and price controls on ethanol, the policy has since lapsed due to improvements in the world sugar market).

In general, there are two strategies for reducing CO_2 emissions – end-use strategies concerned with energy efficiency, and source strategies concerned with the generation of energy from new sources. Battle McCarthy are closely involved in the first strategy – the design of buildings and urban development to minimise energy consumption – and are also carrying out several studies into the use of renewable energy sources. According to the government, renewables in the UK offer a total resource of 150 TWh/year of electricity at a price less than 10 p/kWh (current consumer grid price is 7.5 p/kWh) – 11 per cent of total current demand. About 80 TWh – or 50 per cent – of that total resource is represented by energy crops.

Energy crops are grown to be burnt or gasified to generate electricity and heat, producing energy with a zero or negative CO_2 balance. Burning the crop emits carbon dioxide into the atmosphere, but the growing crop absorbs the same amount of carbon dioxide (the power plant is not running while the first crop is growing, so the carbon budget is always in the black by one crop's worth of CO_2).

In recent decades, energy crops under investigation have included rape seed (used to produce rape seed oil, a diesel replacement) and types of rapid-growing African grass like Miscanthus. Interest is now focused on coppicing, used for hundreds of years to manufacture small-diameter timber. Coppicing involves cutting back young trees just above the roots, and allowing them to sprout back with multiple shoots. The yield is very high (up to 30 tonnes/ha/year), and the process requires a minimum of pest control, fertilisation and general maintenance – so that the financial and environmental costs of management are extremely small when compared with other arable crops. Where traditional coppice had a rotation of 7 to 14 years, the modern version Short Rotation Coppice (SRC) has a rotation of two or three years, with yields about four times higher.

Energy crops also have the following advantages:
– productive and income-generating use of set-aside land;
– creation of structural landscaping;
– planted areas can be used for different types of recreation;
– ecological diversity supported is relatively high compared to arable farming;
– they may be fertilised with digested sewage. Twelve per cent of UK farmland is currently set-aside, most of which would be suited for growing SRC – and farmers would still be eligible for EU set-aside grants to top up the income from SRC. The UK currently has 13 million hectares of farmland, of which about 1.56 million hectares is in set-aside. If all of this were to be used for SRC, then the electricity resource is about 47 TWh a year, equivalent to about 2,500 times the electricity demand for London.

Farming in the UK is amongst the most efficient in the world, a highly mechanised process driven by only three per cent of the population. This efficiency creates agricultural surpluses, but also makes the industry well-adjusted for adaptation to energy crop production with no loss in agricultural productivity. With the necessary vision, energy crops could form a central part of UK energy supply, creating a new structure for the British landscape of the next century.

The authors would like to acknowledge the contribution made by Robert Webb to the preparation of this article.

Straw bales seen being lifted into a CHP plant in Denmark

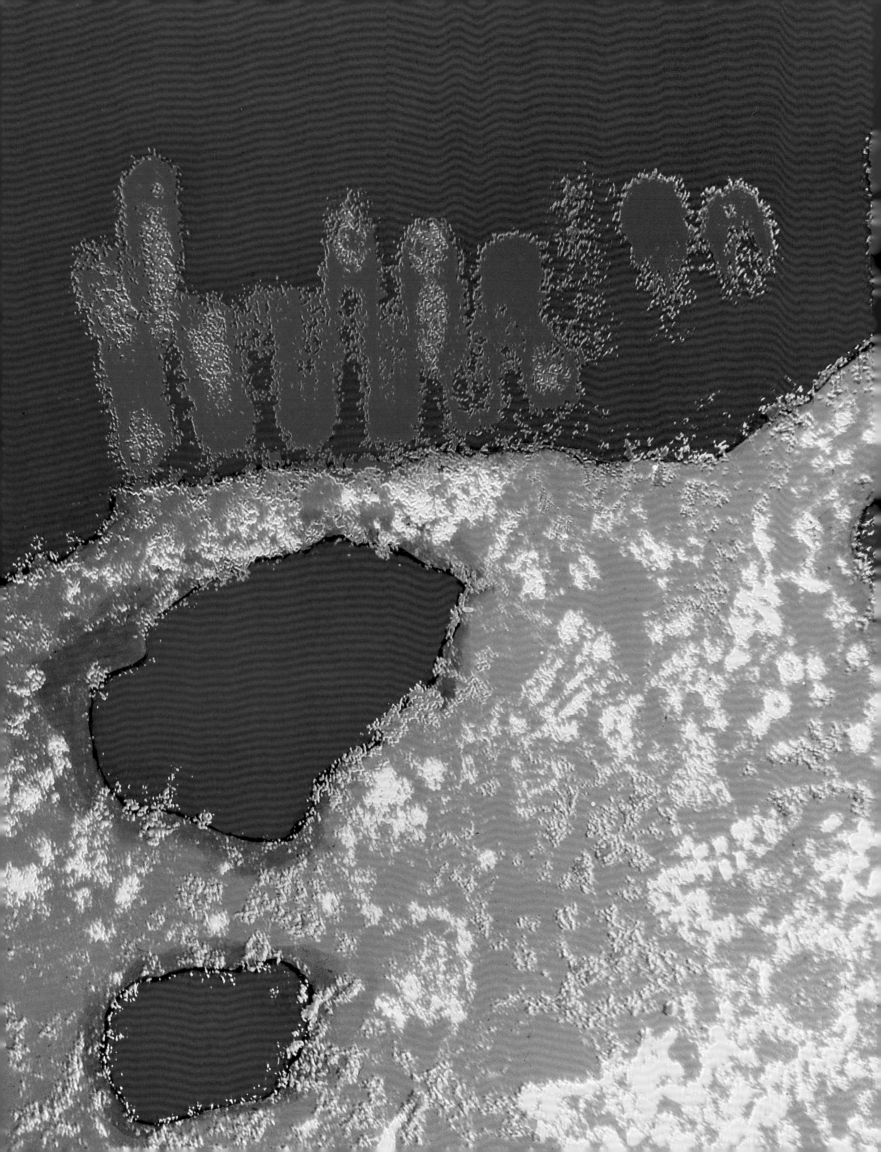

LANDSCAPE SUSTAINED BY NATURE

He leapt the garden wall and saw that all nature was a garden.
Horace Walpole, writing about William Kent, the 18th-century landscape architect.

In the archetypal suburb, wide empty streets are lined by parked cars separated by barren and sterile strips of grass. It is a space largely untouched by human activity; except on Sunday mornings, the time for washing of cars and mowing of lawns. The weekly routine probably serves a social purpose – allowing residents to exhibit themselves and their cars briefly to each other – but is this enough to justify the ecological sterility of those ubiquitous lawns?

Last year the British public spent over £250 million on lawn mowers and other grass-related materials and machines to maintain their private gardens. Taking into account the additional cost of petrol and electricity to run the equipment, together with the considerable industrial, commercial and retail support required, it would appear that the UK is supporting a huge market based purely on keeping grass at an acceptable height and colour. If we also consider the 100,000 acres of local authority parkland and the thousands of miles of road verges throughout the country, we get a picture of a massive human folly. The fuel alone required for the various grass maintenance machines in the UK could probably power a third world city whilst the many hectares of neat and tidy grass represent ecological sterility, destabilising ecosystems and actively contributing to the destruction of biodiversity through the application of pesticides.

This is not a new story and neither is it the most extreme example of how we mismanage our landscape in environmental terms. However, it highlights one of the fundamental problems facing broad acceptance of an ecologically sustainable way of life for all, and that is public taste. In Britain especially we are weighed down by the culture of tidiness and by the negative associations of weeds and rampant nature. Is it conceivable that public taste will stifle sustainability in the same way that it has marginalised architecture?

People have always been fascinated by the difference between wild landscapes and their man-made/constructed counterparts. Some of the most successful man-made landscapes, like those of Capability Brown, were designed as a human interpretation of a natural form whilst the landscapes of power (Versailles, the White House lawn) have consistently tried to subjugate and control nature. The ancient Persian view of nature was more sophisticated: it took in both views, celebrating both the preciousness of the cultivated garden, and the emotive beauty of wilderness.

Underlying this confusion over aesthetics is the lack of understanding of function in landscape. Brown's landscapes were functional in a simple way; employing sheep and cows to keep the grass short and keep tree branches above ground, creating a classic landscape characterised by rolling grass-covered hills dotted with broad-leaved trees of the familiar shape. But we have since forgotten the functional reason for the appearance of this and many other landscape types, and as we try and replicate them without their creating function we have to fall back on the powerful tools of chemicals , machines and energy.

Until recently only the most obvious human-centred functions have been designed for: fields for production of grain, parks for walking the dog, lawns for playing croquet. Each of these landscapes performs its limited human function in the short term, although each is sterile and destructive in its own way. We know that if we continue to alter and simplify the natural order of the planet what's at risk is not the earth itself (which will simply evolve new forms of life and ecological processes), but our own social systems and ultimately our own species. To avoid this self-destruction we must adopt more sustainable systems and for this we need to understand and be able to mimic nature.

To create sustainable landscapes we need to develop a methodology for assessing, planning and designing landscapes that goes well beyond the counting of wildlife species or the judgement of scenic value. The critical currency of the future should be energy – rather than, for instance, monetary value – and environmental judgements should be based on

OPPOSITE: False-colour transmission electron micrograph of a cell infected by influenza virus; courtesy of Dr Gopal Murti/Science Photo Library; FROM ABOVE: One-dimensional human uses of landscape – flower clock being planted in a municipal park; industrial horticulture; landing strip; OVERLEAF: Assessment of landscape types for the Groningen Zuid-Oost site – existing types (left), proposed landscaped types (right). Each 'mark' has been calculated by an ecologist as an assessment of ecological value under each category. The assessment has helped guide decisions about the relative land area and placing of each type in the new framework structure.

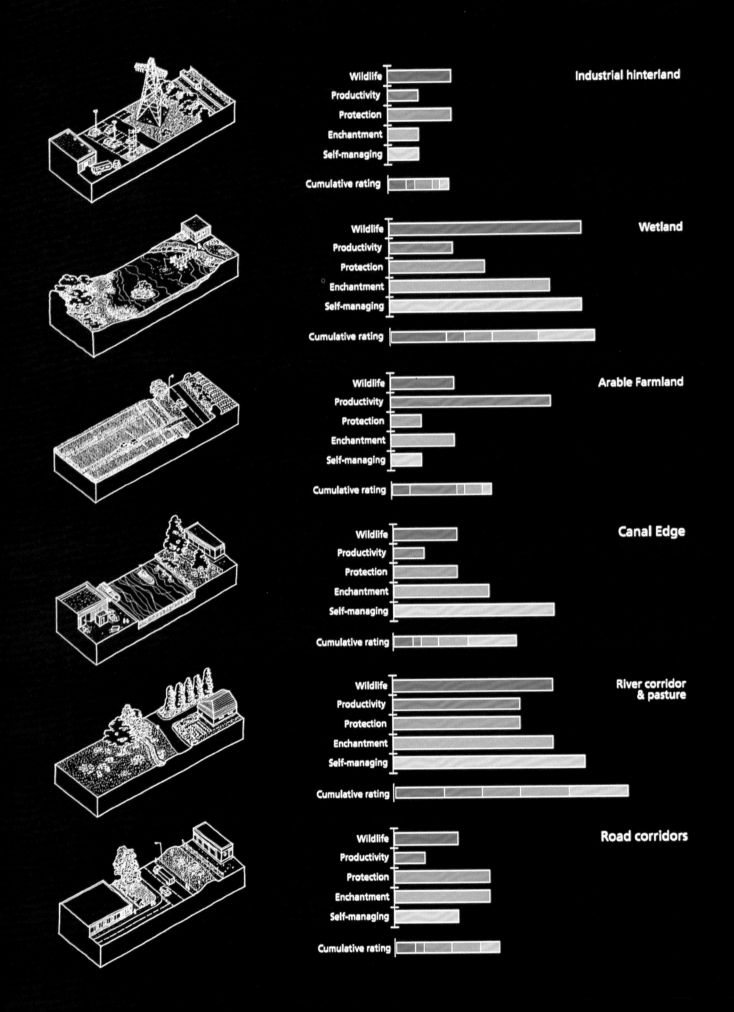

Industrial hinterland

Wildlife
Productivity
Protection
Enchantment
Self-managing

Cumulative rating

Wetland

Wildlife
Productivity
Protection
Enchantment
Self-managing

Cumulative rating

Arable Farmland

Wildlife
Productivity
Protection
Enchantment
Self-managing

Cumulative rating

Canal Edge

Wildlife
Productivity
Protection
Enchantment
Self-managing

Cumulative rating

River corridor & pasture

Wildlife
Productivity
Protection
Enchantment
Self-managing

Cumulative rating

Road corridors

Wildlife
Productivity
Protection
Enchantment
Self-managing

Cumulative rating

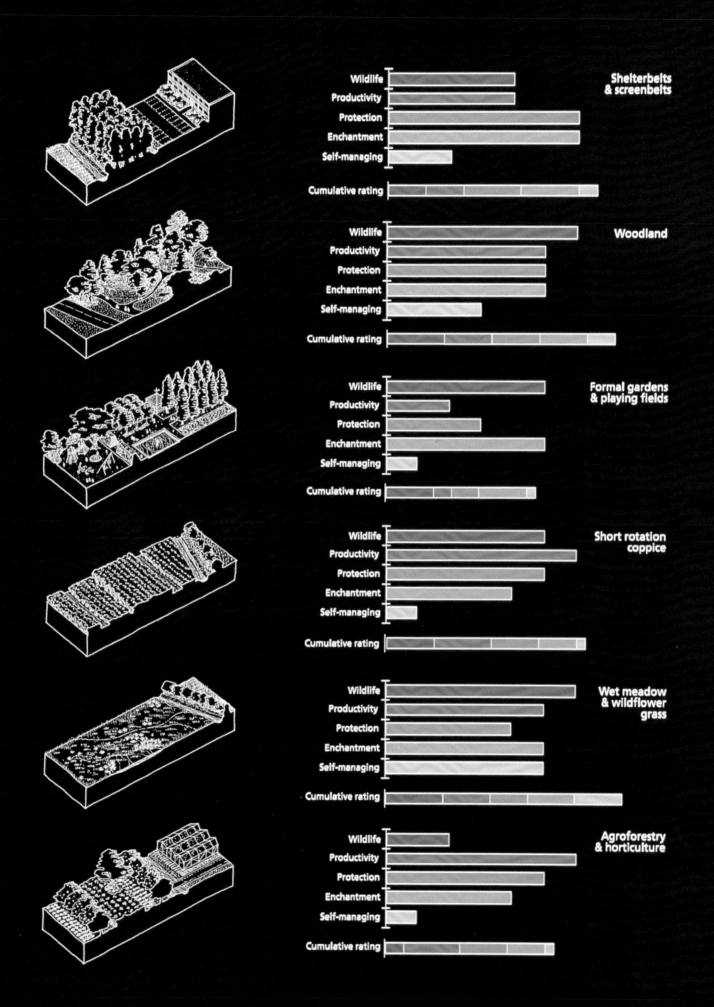

Shelterbelts & screenbelts

- Wildlife
- Productivity
- Protection
- Enchantment
- Self-managing

Cumulative rating

Woodland

- Wildlife
- Productivity
- Protection
- Enchantment
- Self-managing

Cumulative rating

Formal gardens & playing fields

- Wildlife
- Productivity
- Protection
- Enchantment
- Self-managing

Cumulative rating

Short rotation coppice

- Wildlife
- Productivity
- Protection
- Enchantment
- Self-managing

Cumulative rating

Wet meadow & wildflower grass

- Wildlife
- Productivity
- Protection
- Enchantment
- Self-managing

Cumulative rating

Agroforestry & horticulture

- Wildlife
- Productivity
- Protection
- Enchantment
- Self-managing

Cumulative rating

1

2

3

4

5

○ Industrial hinterland

○ Canal strip

◔ River strip

○ Arable

● Woodland

◔ Short rotation coppice

◔ Agroforestry/Horticulture

○ Wetlands

◔ Wet meadow & wildflower grass

◔ Formal gardens

1 Land use on site as existing. The run down industrial area serves the canals taking freight long-distance to Germany. Arable land to the east is designated for development.
2 Phase one of growth to the east of site; landscape structure developed from existing drainage pattern in arable land. Undeveloped sites used to grow short rotation coppice as an energy crop.
3, 4 Phases 2-3 of new growth. Coppice gives way to construction. New woodland connections are created from east to west.
5 East-west connections complete; new pockets of green in the existing industrial area

an assessment of energy balance and energy cycles within a given environment or ecosystem. The ecologist Eugene P Odum worked on this proposition as long ago as the 1960s, and it forms the basis of the landscape design principles now being developed.

Working with project architect Chris Moller and the urban design team of Groningen in the Netherlands, Battle McCarthy has been developing an analysis of this nature for a large industrial area on the south-east edge of the town, known as Zuid-Oost. Here, we have assessed a range of existing and proposed landscape types under three principal headings: production; protection; and enchantment.

Productive landscapes

We can measure the capacity of a landscape to do productive work and we can plan the landscape to maximise its efficient use and productivity. Landscape productivity could be considered under the following headings: Oxygen production; Carbon dioxide absorption; Waste treatment; Food production; Timber production; Wildlife diversity; Movement of resources; Energy potential; Recreational resource; Healthy environment; Added quality of life; Added commercial value; and Employment potential.

Productive landscape components can be considered as those that most closely represent forest edge habitat - a combination of open and enclosed spaces, a mixture of trees and ground cover. These areas are suggestive of a safe landscape, managed and used by people. They can be planned and designed to reinforce these qualities.

Protective landscape

Landscape components can also protect people and buildings. We can measure the protective value of landscape under the following headings: Shelter and climate moderation; Absorbtion of pollution; Prevention of flooding; Security; Conservation of natural and historic features; Screening of undesirable elements; Providing a framework for planning and economic initiatives.

Protective landscape components could reflect the wilder, more natural character of climax woodland or extensive wetlands and marshes. They are the buffers between the productive landscapes and they could suggest a natural dominance with a hint of danger.

Enchanting landscape

We normally associate landscapes with their scenic and visual qualities but rarely with other subjective associations that include: Mood and character; Sensory appeal; Cultural association; Intellectual stimulation; Gut responses.

Enchanting landscape components could provide cultural landmarks within the new productive and protective landscapes. They could become the focus of communities within this ecological landscape matrix.

Landscapes sustained by nature

The work at Groningen is only the first step towards developing a vibrant ecological structure plan for the area, and it is only an early move in the analysis required to support the design of sustainable landscapes. Designers must search for the optimum 'ecological' equation that best suits each site, consult the genius of the place, and develop elegant solutions predicated on the uniqueness of place. In some instances the preference may be for considerable intervention and management, elsewhere there may be a shift towards a regulated nature and in other places we may remove our influence completely. Landscapes of the future will not be judged by their political, scenic or even monetary worth alone but on their inherent ecological potential and on the sustainability of the energy flows within each given site, district, ecosystem or biome.

Ultimately, the challenge is to find a balance between simplified human ecosystems and their more complex, natural neighbours, and to find ways of sustaining our environment and landscape using the ecological efficiency of nature. As our understanding of ecology increases, the constantly changing shape of our landscapes will provide a litmus test for our developing design skill.

The authors would like to thank Andrew Grant and Robert Webb for their assistance with the preparation of this article.

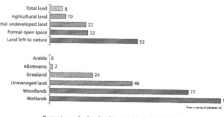

Percentage of urban land types with ecological value

OPPOSITE: The ecological and landscape strategy for the development of Groningen, phased drawings; ABOVE: The integration of nature and technology; graph showing the relative ecological value of different urban land types, from a study of Leicester.

TOWARDS THE LIGHT

He saw; but blasted with excess of light
Closed his eyes in endless night.
Thomas Gray, *Elegy in a Churchyard*

An increase in the intensity of light is not what
we need. It is already much too strong, and can
no longer be tolerated by our eyes. Tempered
light is what we need. Not 'More light' but 'More
coloured light!' must be the call . . . Colour-
tempered light settles the nerves, and it is used
by neurologists as an element in the cures at
their sanatoria . . .
Paul Scheerbart, *Glasarchitektur*, 1914

The science of light and the technology of its manipulation is highly advanced. We can create lasers to destroy missiles in space or make tiny incisions in human tissue, and control the emission of single protons, yet our understanding of the human response to light is simplistic and poorly researched. Conventional lighting design aims only to achieve sufficient illumination at the minimum cost, ignoring its influence on mood, perception and comfort.

Lighting design or analysis is too often an afterthought to the design of a building, when it could be the generator of form. Light creates space and emotion, and should be one of the principal media of the architect engineer. The future of architecture is sculpting in light.

Electromagnetic spectrum

The electromagnetic spectrum ranges from gamma and X-rays at the short end of the spectrum to radio waves and Extremely Low Frequency waves (ELF) used for submarine communication. In the centre is the range of wavelengths that our eyes are sensitive to, the visible spectrum; from 3.8×10^{-7}m (blue) to 7.6×10^{-7}m (red). Beyond blue is ultraviolet which can damage the skin, whilst beyond red is infra-red, or radiant heat.

Electromagnetic radiation consists of fluctuations in the electric and magnetic fields, which take place at right angles to each other. Like ripples in a pond, disturbances in the electromagnetic field spread out from the source. All electromagnetic waves move at the same speed (299,792 kms) but travel more slowly through different materials (glass 198,223kms).

The human eye is our passport to this world. The retina contains 6.5 million cones, responsive to colour and intensity, and 125 million rods which are more sensitive but perceive only the quality of light not its hue. There are more cones at the centre of the field of vision and more rods at its periphery, explaining why during periods of low illumination objects are brighter in the peripherals than the centre.

We can perceive a huge range of light levels. The rods begin operating at a surface luminance of 0.001cd/m^2 (candelas per metre squared), at 3cd/m^2 the cones start operating and at 1,000cd/m^2 the pupil closes down to its minimum. To put these into perspective the full moon emits 2,500cd/m^2, the filament of a standard incandescent light 7,000,000cd/m^2 and the surface of the sun 1,650,000,000cd/m^2.

Human response

In Sweden, at the beginning of every dark winter, more and more people start to make a daily trip to the local medical centre, to sit for 30 minutes dressed entirely in white in a bright room flooded with 10,000 lux of daylight-spectrum light. These individuals are sufferers from Seasonally Affective Disorder (SAD), a recently recognised phenomenon. Without light therapy, SAD sufferers become depressed, tired and irritable when the winter sets in and daylight hours drop below a certain level. SAD is thought to be linked to the pituitary gland – the 'third eye' which controls key body functions including sleep and the perception of time – and is an interesting example of how light influences the way we feel and perceive.

Human responses to light vary with climate, culture and the individual. For most people, red light is 'warm' and blue light is 'cold'. However people from Southern Europe will be more comfortable on a hot day in a dark or shuttered room, whilst people from Northern Europe would rather be in a warming bright light.

Researchers have discovered that fluctuating illumination in the workplace throughout the day influences productivity; greater production can be achieved by gradually raising the intensity of lighting at certain times. Similarly, at the centre of deep plan buildings lighting is maintained at higher levels than near to the windows, to compensate for the lack of perceived daylight.

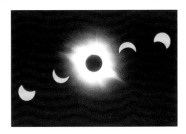

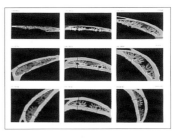

FROM ABOVE: Sequential photographs of lunar eclipse; solar analysis, Holy Island, with Andrew Wright; solar analysis, L'lle Seguin, with Richard Rogers Partnership

Lighting design

Lighting is conventionally designed to provide a constant specified light level at the working plane, with the spacing and layout of luminaires being determined through simple calculations. More recently the reduction of energy use, through the maximisation of daylighting, has become a priority as lighting accounts for up to 20 per cent of the electrical demands for an average building. This approach involves plan depths of between 12 and 15 metres, carefully designed windows and shading systems and the use of 'intelligent' computer controls linked to dimmer switches and external lighting sensors, but can reduce lighting energy use by 60 per cent or more.

There is a variety of new and existing tools which allow the design team greater freedom to explore the uses of lighting within their buildings, but despite this the majority of designers still rely on more traditional methods. The analysis of crude cardboard models under an artificial sky – even though they reproduce a mere 10,000 lux, the 'Standard CIE overcast sky' – and the heliodon, which provides a simple mechanical method to observe sunlight penetration and shadows, remain the most popular tools used during the early stages of the design process. However, much more powerful computer-based applications are being evolved which enable dynamic three-dimensional and generative modelling.

The software programme RADIANCE can be used to provide accurate predictions of daylight levels – plotted as points or contours within space and photorealistic renderings of interiors and exteriors – for different times of the day and year, as well as varying weather conditions. Animation can be used to watch the sun's movement through a space over a year, or the penetration of shadows into external spaces. Alternatively the viewer can assume the viewpoint of the sun and fly over their building, generating a direct appreciation of the effectiveness of shading devices or solar reflectors.

Working on a variety of projects, Battle McCarthy is applying combinations of computer tools enabling the architects to sculpt in light. For the Tate Gallery, Bankside (with Alsop and Störmer) a mixture of simple and intuitive analysis was used to develop a series of 'paintings' exploring the impact that internal variations in light and temperature would have on the visitor. The firm proposed that the illumination of each new gallery, projecting through the redundant box of the power station, could respond to its proximity to the river, external wind speed or even the colour balance of paintings and sculptures.

For the National Glass Centre (with Gollifer Associates), light transmitting materials and associated technologies were used to manipulate lighting; including photochromic, thermochromic and electrochromic materials, holographic glazing and electroluminescent displays. The building will perform its function as an exhibition centre for glass as much in its materials and form as in the displays which occupy its spaces.

Generative modelling

The next step will be to use generative models. If a designer's primary interest is the manipulation of human experience through light, these programmes will enable him to generate hundreds of different forms, in response to a three-dimensional model of illumination and colour; as these proposals are modified so the shape of the building will alter. The building becomes a 'back projection' with emitted photons defining a building on their way to rejoining the sun. This generation of computers will allow the designer to visualise and walk through light as solid objects or mist . . . where the visible becomes invisible. The light flooding through an opening becomes a swelling form to be manipulated.

Even now the lighting designers for 'raves' are pushing back traditional barriers, utilising light and music to create space and heighten the senses. Hopefully in the future architects will learn from this, creating three-dimensional 'lightforms'; specifying colours and intensities based on an understanding of mood.

We have only just begun to ask the questions that lead to a true understanding of light, and to progress any further designers must begin to explore human interaction with different colours and intensities; its influence on mood, and our perception of space, temperature, time and comfort. Lighting design briefs must extend beyond the prosaic minimum specification, inviting architects to sculpt light as they do space.

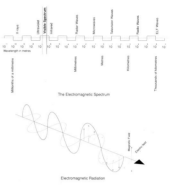

FROM ABOVE: Visible light is a small part of the total electromagnetic spectrum, whose wavelength varies from millionths of millimetres (X-rays) to thousands of kilometres; heliodon used to model solar penetration; analysis of drawing office; computer analysis of light output from one source

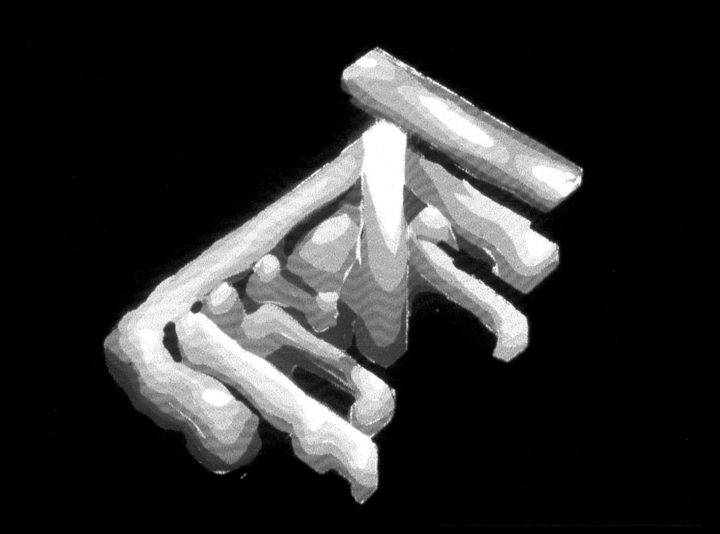

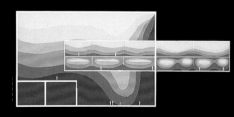
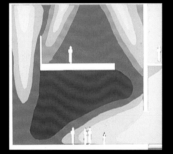

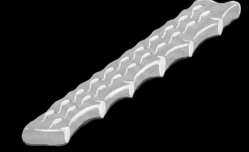

Competition entry for the new Tate at Bankside, with Alsop & Störmer. Based on simple and intuitive analysis, a series of drawings was produced to explore the idea of sculpting in light, so that the experience of the visitor is to wander through a constantly changing set of light and temperature experiences, responding to the location of the gallery and the type of works shown. ABOVE: Drawing of daylight levels in the overall form; FROM L TO R: Model of proposal; lighting studies

OPPOSITE ABOVE: Daylight analysis; OPPOSITE BELOW: Daylighting analysis for Bluewater retail development, with Eric Kuhne & Associates, carried out with Integrated Environmental Solutions using RADIANCE. The objective has been to create a shopping street with a similar variation in environmental conditions to an external street, but without the drawbacks of weather and cold. Daylighting is one of the environmental variables that the design team has to balance against temperature, air movement, and energy use to create a successful design. For example, the desire for a daylit space creates the requirement for 60 per cent of the roof to be glazed, but this creates a higher cooling requirement and makes it more difficult to naturally ventilate the space. In this case it is more energy efficient to reduce the amount of glazing and rely on electric light than to increase the cooling load.

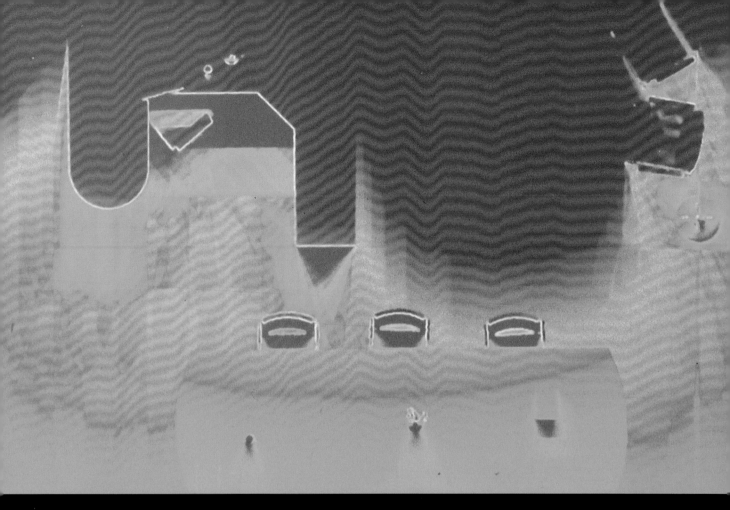

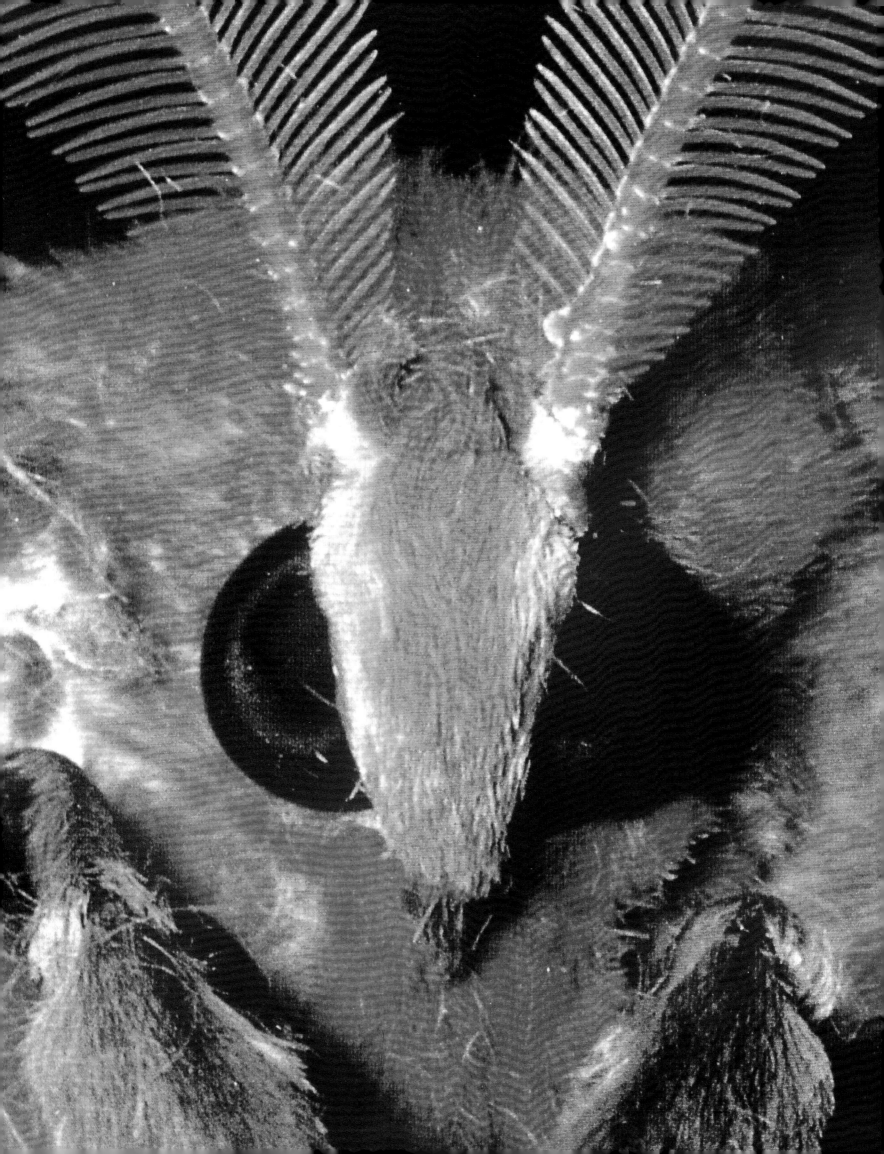

AN ARCHITECTURE OF SMELL

*Smells and tastes . . . alone, more fragile but
more enduring, more insubstantial, more
persistent . . . bear unflinchingly, in the tiny and
almost impalpable drop of their essence, the
vast structure of recollection.*
Marcel Proust, *Remembrance of Things Past*

*And so he would now study perfumes . . . He saw
that there was no mood of the mind that had not
its counterpart in the sensuous life, and set
himself to discover their true relations, wondering
what there was in frankincense that made one
mystical, and in ambergris that stirred one's
passions, and in violets that woke the memory of
dead romances, and in musk that troubled the
brain, and in champak that stained the imagination; and seeking often to elaborate a real psychology of perfumes, and to estimate the several
influences of sweet-smelling roots, and scented
pollen-laden flowers, or aromatic balms, and of
dark and fragrant woods, of spikenard that
sickens, of hovenia that makes men mad, and of
aloes that are said to be able to expel melancholy
from the soul.*
Oscar Wilde, *The Picture of Dorian Gray*

Smells and fragrances have always
played a critical role in human affairs
but, of all the senses, smell is the least
researched and understood. In fact, over the
last 2,000 years, its perceived importance has
been gradually undermined by a combination
of cultural conceit and odour pollution.

But smell is undergoing a renaissance.
Engineers are relatively skilled in the design of
visual and acoustic environments, even if only
to satisfy functional requirements. However,
designers are now creating olfactory environments; places where smell is used to create
emotion, recollection and mood.

Smell is arguably the most subtle and
powerful sense in its potential for emotional
impact. Humans can recognise 10,000 different
odours, each of which has distinct characteristics and associations for each individual. Smells
can induce fear, desire or joy, defining our
experience of space in often unconscious ways.

The science of smell
Odour is our response to molecular compounds
of varying size and structure. The smell receptors
are tiny hairs, or cilia, on neurones located in
the olfactory epithelium of the nasal cavity.
These neurones are the only direct physical
connection between the external world and the
brain as they are in constant contact with
inhaled air. Odour molecules bind to receptor
proteins on the cilia which stimulate a tiny
electrical charge along axons to the olfactory
bulbs in the brain.

Each odour consists of a mixture of many
different chemicals, though the perception is of
one distinct smell rather than a series of individual components. Different neurones respond
to different chemicals, so that each odour has its
own pattern of responding neurones; forming a
particular image inside the brain.

The psychology of smell is extremely complex as odours are processed in the part of the
brain concerned with emotional response.
Hence, individuals respond differently to the
same odours, with sensitivity varying with time
and age, as well as mood. Similarly women are
more sensitive to smells than men and certain
people are able to ignore particular odours
after prolonged exposure.

The impact of smells can be directly measured by recording electrical activity in the brain
in relation to exposure. Upward shifts in brainwave activity have been measured after exposure to jasmine or peppermint oil, indicating a
stimulating effect, whilst oils such as lavender
or sandalwood produce a downward shift,
indicating a sedative effect. Research in this
area is still in its early stages, though it prom-
ises to map one of the most unexplored areas
of human knowledge.

Towards an architecture of smell
Current attempts to use smell in architecture
are crude and usually focused on the single
goal of selling; supermarkets pumping the
smell of freshly baked bread into their lobbies
to lure customers in. However, there are a few
examples of more inventive application. In
Japan, firms are using fragrance to increase
worker productivity, using a variety of odours
throughout the day. Citrus and peppermint
smells are used to counteract early morning or
afternoon fatigue, and wood smells are used at
lunch to underline the fact that it is time to rest.

Smells can be used to construct a physical

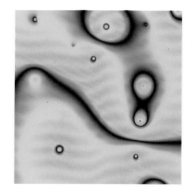

*OPPOSITE: The most acute
sense of smell exhibited in nature
is that of the male emperor moth
(Eudia Pavonia) which according
to German experiments carried
out in 1961, can detect the sex
attractant of the virgin female at a
range of 11km upwind. The scent
has been identified as one of the
higher alcohols ($C_{16}H_{29}OH$), of
which the female carries less
than 0.0001mg; ABOVE: Computer visualisation of scent contours
diffusing through space.*

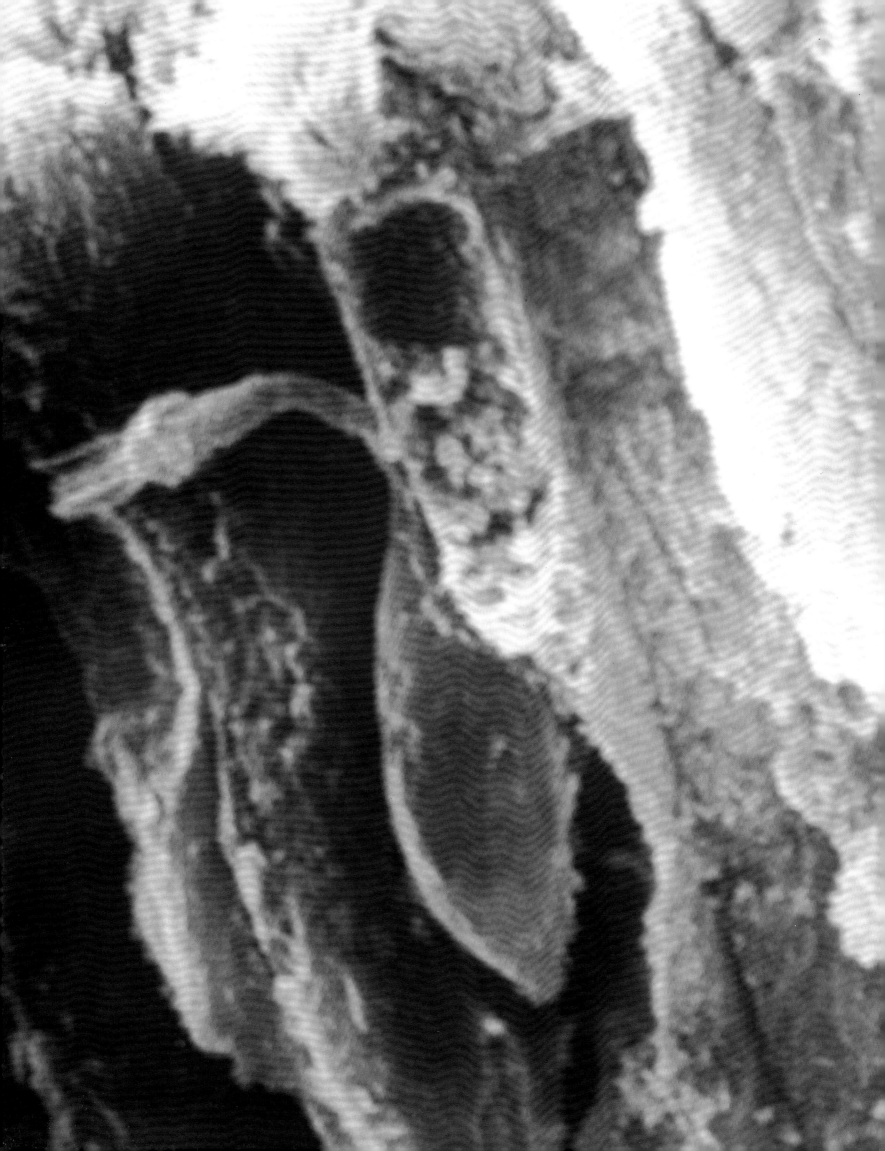

architecture in the same way that light and sound can be used to sculpt or define space. Smells can form olfactory barriers – working like mosquito repellents – or tempting trails. One of the most famous odour experiments involves pheromones (human sexual scents). Women or men entering a waiting-room have been observed to repeatedly choose to sit in the chair that has been sprayed with the pheromone of the opposite sex, even when all others remain unoccupied.

Public spaces should have a celebratory architecture of smell. Temples and churches still use fragrance to lift the spirit and transform the everyday, while modern secular spaces have opted for a democratic blandness. Instead they should be vibrant and replete with scent. In the past this was woven into the fabric of the building itself to ensure an aromatic atmosphere; early Indian temples were constructed entirely from sandalwood, and to the mortar of their temples the Babylonians added perfume. Today, modern approaches are more likely to be software-based, with air handling systems and dedicated equipment generating and distributing smell.

Using software-based odour generation, public spaces could be filled with constantly varying olfactory environments, ebbing and flowing in response to the season, time of day or weather, or to any other combination of variables; the actions and movements of visitors; the inputs of a million people via the internet, or a model of the world stock market.

Design with odour
Although humans can distinguish between many thousands of different odours, they lack the appropriate vocabulary to describe or draw them, hindering attempts to integrate olfaction into the design process. Wine-tasters and other odour professionals have had to define their own language, and the unit of smell, the Olf, can only be defined by experts specially trained for the purpose. In Scandinavia 'Sensory Panels' are employed by the government to monitor the air quality standard in buildings by carrying out olfactory inspections of the interior spaces on a regular basis. Eventually these smell specialists will become as vital to designers as lightmeters and thermometers.

Unfortunately these methods are devised with the intention of analysing existing odours rather than producing an aromatic palette. Instead, it seems likely that a system of colour-coded analysis – used today for the representation of light and sound – will be developed enabling designers to create and communicate proposals for specific olfactory environments. The designer will be able to select from an infinite range of smells randomly generated by computer, and evolve new combinations of scents by the mixing and mating of components. Other methods will rely on more intuitive and evolutionary techniques.

The use of aromatic herbs and essential oils dates back to the early days of civilisation. Smells have been used as anti-depressants, euphorics, sedatives, aphrodisiacs and more, but the future of olfactory architecture will surpass these definitions. We do not know how many smells remain to be discovered.

The authors would like to thank Karin Galster and Robert Webb for their assistance with the preparation of this article.

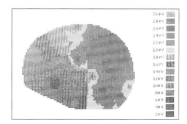

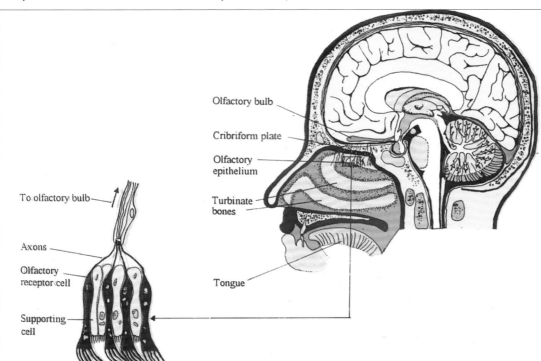

OPPOSITE: A sensory neuron in the human olfactory epithelium, surrounded by support cells. The hair-like cilia which carry the receptors can be seen protruding from its tip; FROM ABOVE: The physiology of smell; graph of recorded shifts in brainwave patterns in response to certain essential oils; BEAM scan of the brain responding to a smell identified as pleasant – the right hemisphere showing increased electrical activity.

DYNAMIC CITIES

The nature of our cities and towns defines the qualities of civilisation itself. Yet at present their development is a stilted and haphazard process of change, responding to the skewed objectives of individual pressures rather than the functional organic growth of the whole.

We separate the producer from the consumer, the farmer from the kitchen, the power plant from the appliance, the dump site from the garbage can, the banker from the borrower and depositor, and inevitably, the government from the citizenry. Development becomes a process by which we separate authority and responsibility, where those who make decisions are not affected by the decisions.

Morris, quoted in *Reviving the City*
There are two challenges for the design and management of cities in the 21st century. First, the functions and operation of urban areas must be better understood, so that cities can work at maximum efficiency. Second, the process of design and decision-making must be developed to address a broad base of constituencies and needs: social, economic and environmental.

The form of cities has always been driven by the interaction of certain critical forces: the market, or the need to trade; patterns and technologies of movement; the distribution and availability of energy; the supply and distribution of water; the safe and effective disposal of waste, and the availability of natural resources. A number of analysis tools are currently being evolved which will help people to consider all of these elements as part of the public discussion to shape the development of cities. This progress is contemporaneous with the application of participative design, which ensures that the widest range of issues are considered during the design process, and that when proposals do emerge, they can proceed with the support and contributions of the citizens.

Battle McCarthy have recently taken part in such a process in the town of Zaanstad, on the northern periphery of Amsterdam. The chief planner, Miranda Reitsma, was asked to prepare a set of proposals for a problematic and undeveloped area to the west of the town centre. Unwilling to tackle such a difficult site with conventional planning techniques, she invited Chris Moller of Studio 333 to help set up a new process based on design workshops. The objective was to create a resilient and

flexible framework for future development on the site and discover the catalysts of infrastructure required to set it in motion. The workshops were organised around three themes, recognised early on as critical for the success of any proposals to the site: movement; landscape and ecology, and diversification of use.

A range of people, from within the local authority and external consultancies, were invited to join the process. At each workshop, traffic engineers, landscape ecologists and building and urban designers were invited to describe their own objectives for the area, and to participate in explorations of the range of potential solutions.

The organisers set out to make a range of tools available to the workshop groups so that each issue could be properly investigated and understood. Working with two postgraduate groups from the Bartlett School of Architecture, University College London, the participants were able to apply two relevant computer programs: Space Syntax, to understand movement, and Pangea, a 3D sketch design tool used here to investigate building density and use.

The following pages illustrate and describe the analysis carried out in the workshops, and the outline proposals arising from the work, presented under a series of headings: 'Movement', 'Urban Mix', 'Ecology and Water', and 'Synthesis'. The process is still ongoing, and it is hoped that further tools will be developed and applied as the design progresses.

Information on Space Syntax and Pangea is available on the internet at the following addresses:
  http://doric.bart.ucl.ac.uk/web/slab/slabhome.html
  http://doric.bart.ucl.ac.uk/web/Pangea/
  Intelligent Architecture
The Intelligent Architecture project is funded by DTi and EPSRC. Funding collaborators on the project are: Avanti Architects Ltd, Bovis Construction Ltd, Broadgate Properties Ltd, Criterion Software Ltd, DEGW London Ltd, Oscar Faber Consultant Ltd, PowerGen PLC, Richard Rogers Partnership, Small-World Systems Ltd, Qualum Ltd, UCL Bartlett and UCL Computer Science.

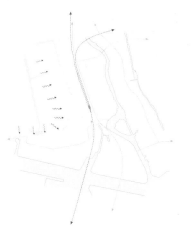

OPPOSITE: The East End of London drawn by Booth in the 1890s; INSERTS, FROM ABOVE: Movement; urban mix; built form; synthesis; FROM ABOVE: Site analysis; typical view of wetlands to the west

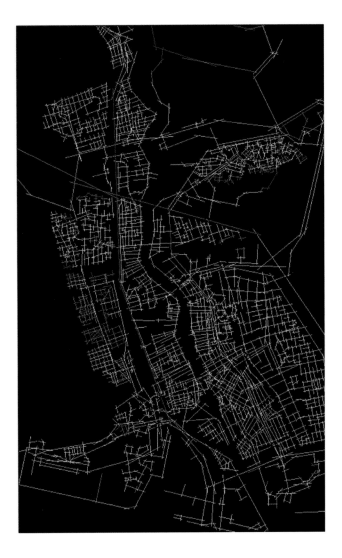

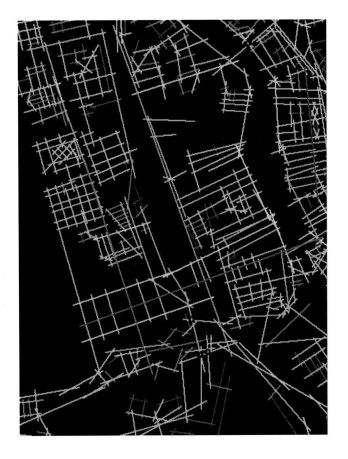

Analysis carried out at the workshops, using the Space Syntax tool, was critical to the design group's understanding of the site.

FROM ABOVE, LEFT TO RIGHT: Axial map of Zaanstad showing global integration. The road and railway line at the centre of the town create a clear break between the east and west sides; Early model of the site with sketch proposal developed at the workshop. Routes are created across the railway increasing the integration of the west side; Extending the existing high street across the railway, to the west extends the 'strip effect'. As more connections are established, a locally intelligible district begins to emerge.

Zaanstad
MOVEMENT

Movement is central to the operation and shape of cities. As Jane Jacobs pointed out, it is likely that urbanisation itself developed as a result of movement through trade, as early man began to realise that a resource which was plentiful and cheap in onc location could be rare and valuable somewhere else. The most successful early conurbations were those located at the crossing of trade routes, places where people could interact and barter. The primary purpose of cities, and what makes them dynamic places, is essentially the same, and the heart of a successful city is a bustling street.

There are many theories of how people move through cities. The controversial theorist Kevin Lynch has argued that urban navigation and movement is guided by visual and cultural landmarks. There is also a common assumption that key activities can be located relatively independently of spatial patterns. However, the research of Professor Bill Hillier, and others at the Bartlett, has demonstrated that layout is at least as important in directing movement as any other factor. They have also developed a mathematical modelling tool, Space Syntax, to calculate the 'integration' of each space within a city; the accessibility of each space from every other space in the system. Studies have shown a strong relationship between integration and levels of movement in urban areas.

The analysis has the advantage that it is immediate and visual – categorising well integrated spaces as warm, or red, and the least integrated spaces as cool, or blue – and is ideal for participative design. At Zaanstad it was possible to test different proposals for the town and site in a very short time. Each graphic model is supported by a statistical database, which allows users to pick out new lines of movement, within a scattergram of the whole, and examine its spatial properties in detail.

The design proposals, based on this analysis, involve extending the existing shopping street across the railway to the west, enhancing its 'strip effect' as a strong, well-integrated space. The railway station at the centre of this route provides excellent connections to the centre of Amsterdam and the surrounding region. The extended space forms a spine to the new development, and secondary streets begin to define the likely building massing.

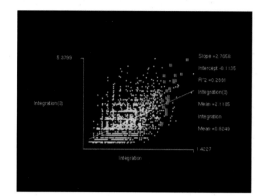

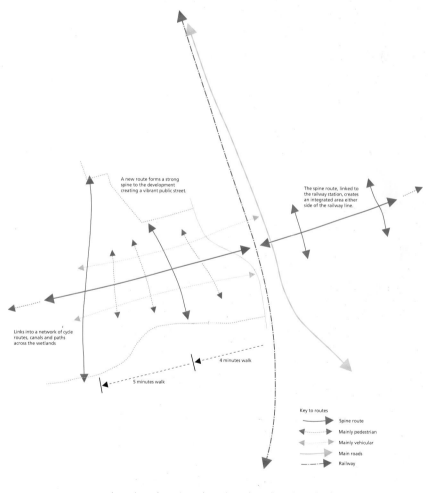

A new route forms a strong spine to the development creating a vibrant public street.

The spine route, linked to the railway station, creates an integrated area either side of the railway line.

Links into a network of cycle routes, canals and paths across the wetlands

4 minutes walk

5 minutes walk

Key to routes

→ Spine route

→ Mainly pedestrian

→ Mainly vehicular

→ Main roads

→ Railway

0m 100m 200m 300m 400m 500m 600m 700m 800m 900m 1km

FROM ABOVE, LEFT TO RIGHT: Aerial view of Oxford Street in central London, an example of a strong route; Scattergram of the Zaanstad proposal, with key routes highlighted in red, illustrating the effect of a strong central route; Movement strategy proposed for the site

Zaanstad
URBAN MIX

Cities are shaped by what people do in them. Each activity has implications for the types of building and spaces, and the people who occupy them. The diversity of activities is critical, affecting value and hence development quality, social mix, population densities and levels of crime, as well as many issues to do with infrastructure sizing, cost and sustainability.

For Zaanstad, a sketch design tool was required which would allow people to investigate possible arrangements of building types and begin to understand how this affects the quality of development and sustainability. This can be carried out with a spreadsheet program, but this would be of only limited usefulness without the limitations of a site and an understanding of the urban consequences.

The Intelligent Architecture project at the Bartlett has been developing software which allows a 3D modelling and viewing program to link into a range of other applications. The program, Pangea, provides a powerful basic tool for a huge range of possible applications, and aims to enable an integrated platform for tasks from design to management.

Pangea's advantage is its robustness and simplicity. Its user interface is direct and intuitive, avoiding the complications of CAD, so that anyone can use it. It allows the participants to sketch in 3D, alter and tweak objects and move around in the environment created. Each object has the potential for simple intelligence.

The simple model developed for the first stage of the exercise was informed by the relationship between movement and building densities. Every building is modelled as a 3D object which knows its designated use and floor area. This is linked to a speadsheet which works out the expected daily and annual profiles for population, electricity and heating. As the user explores the development, the user can select blocks, change use, size or height, and observe how this changes the spreadsheet graphs. The program also colours the model to provide a direct visual interpretation of energy demand and occupation over time.

The designers intend to extend the model, to include land values and rental, so that a social charter can be established. Once an acceptable diversity of occupation and activity is achieved, it will be possible to demonstrate, for example, how higher value development can be used to balance the cost of social housing and maintain a high quality of public space.

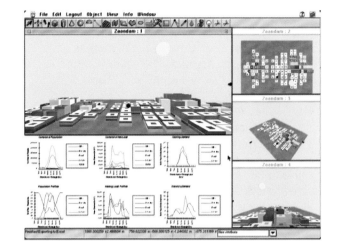

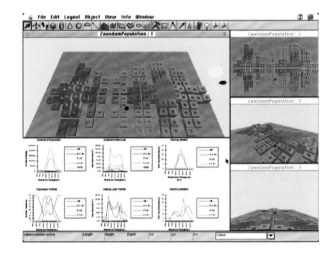

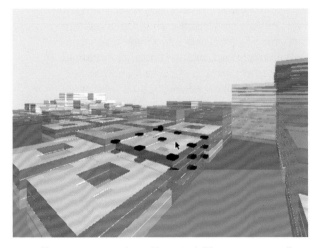

Pangea screen views Zaanstad. The user can walk around the model and change the use and size of blocks, while the daily energy demand, movement and population profiles are plotted on a series of graphs. The objective of achieving a good mix of uses is to even out load profiles.

Zaanstad
WATER AND ECOLOGY

Any process of urbanisation affects the surrounding landscape and wildlife. The task of careful design is to minimise such impact, and to create ecological niches where they did not exist before. The Zaanstad site is partially developed and has little wildlife or ecological value. However, the wetlands to the west are an area of regional importance, providing a habitat for migrant species of bird and a wide range of insects. It was a priority that the national value of the site should provide a special character for the development.

The wetlands themselves are reclaimed land, being used historically for dairy and sheep farming, and it is this combination of activities which has created its unique ecology. Unfortunately, farming is no longer profitable on the land, which is increasingly under-used. It is the objective of the Zaanstad development to instigate an increased, but carefully managed, level of public access to the wetlands, maintaining the momentum and investment required to protect the area.

Areas appropriate for the preservation of wildlife are in many ways described by an inverse of the movement analysis; where people do not go, nature is undisturbed. The effect of the proposed infrastructure would be to make it possible to create an ecological corridor into the town from the wetlands, a transitional zone from urban park to nature.

The water of the wetlands is slightly brackish, a rare quality contributing to its ecological value. Therefore the control of pollution is essential. As well as a system of recycling 'grey water' in buildings to reduce consumption, the designers have proposed the use of biologically based water treatment systems, integrated with the landscape immediately surrounding the new buildings, to purify surface water from roofs and streets before it is allowed to enter the wetlands. This zone of ponds, reed beds and marshes forms a buffer between the wetlands and the development, both physically and visually.

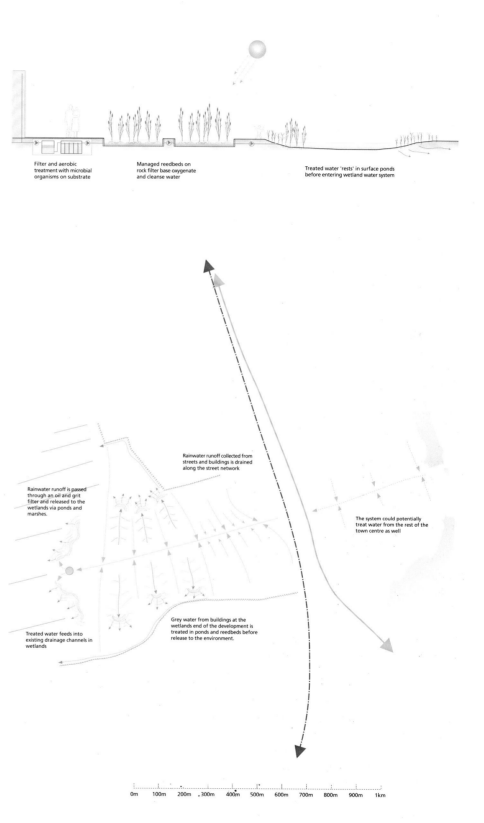

Filter and aerobic treatment with microbial organisms on substrate

Managed reedbeds on rock filter base oxygenate and cleanse water

Treated water 'rests' in surface ponds before entering wetland water system

Rainwater runoff is passed through an oil and grit filter and released to the wetlands via ponds and marshes.

Rainwater runoff collected from streets and buildings is drained along the street network

The system could potentially treat water from the rest of the town centre as well

Treated water feeds into existing drainage channels in wetlands

Grey water from buildings at the wetlands end of the development is treated in ponds and reedbeds before release to the environment.

0m 100m 200m 300m 400m 500m 600m 700m 800m 900m 1km

FROM ABOVE: Proposed surface water treatment system; proposed surface water strategy

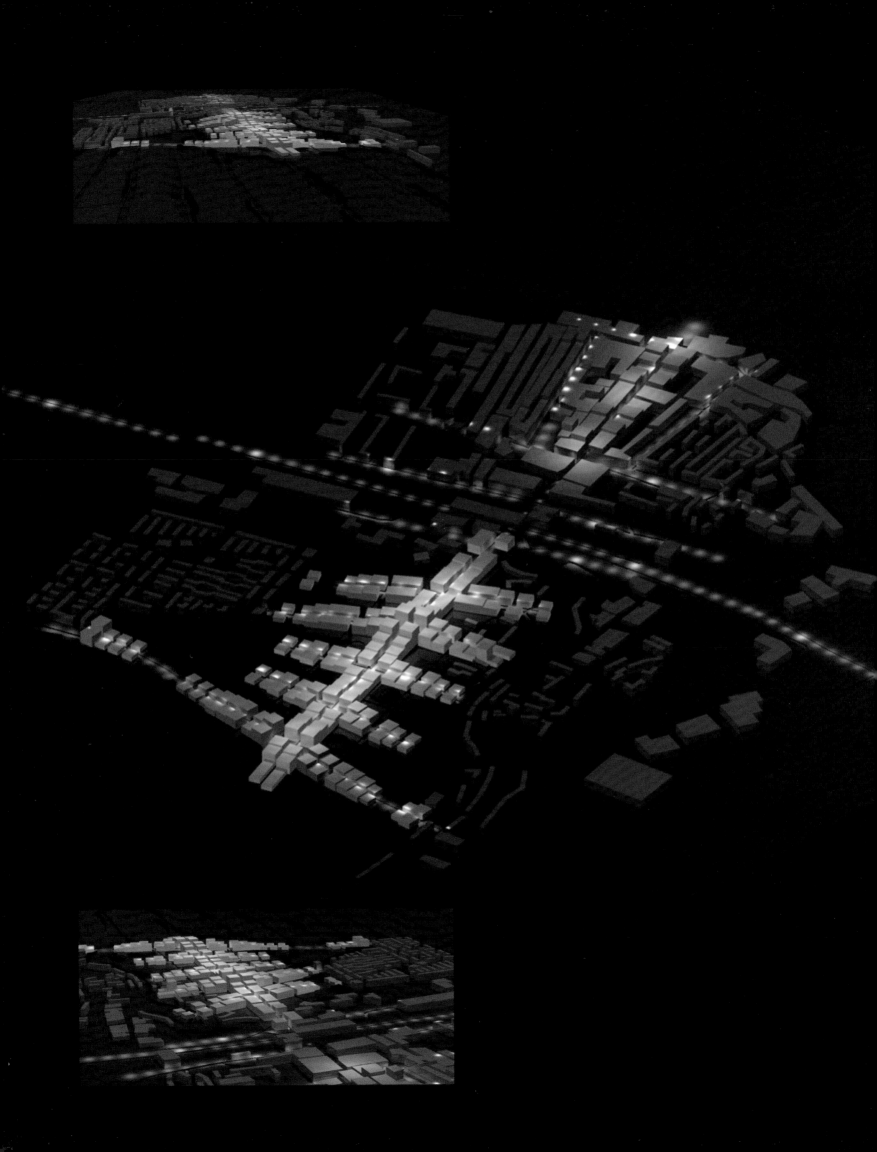

Zaanstad
SYNTHESIS

The process and the tools used here demonstrate some basic principles with the potential for future development. At the heart of this approach is a belief that a firm understanding of functional and engineering principles can lead to the development of rational and successful form. Ensuring a robust strategy for fundamental issues such as movement and energy makes the city work better and increases its sustainability, allowing form and quality to arise directly from specific local conditions. Bringing engineering and design disciplines together can overcome specialist disputes and create a coherent intent. It can reduce infrastructure costs, minimise environmental impact and help ensure a multifaceted design solution whose complexity reflects that of reality.

At Zaanstad, the generation of the proposals is a response to the nature of the site. Movement and ecology have encountered each other and tried to reach an equilibrium. This has suggested form.

Perhaps the most important principle is that the city is for people. Maintaining a vibrant urban environment and public realm is critical to the health of civilisation. There is a need for design tools and processes which allow people to participate in decision-making, to understand the engineering issues involved, and to sketch creatively and observe the implications of different options. Tools such as Pangea and Space Syntax are the first generation of these. But this approach also offers the opportunity for a wider social and economic vision to be developed.

Past attempts to consider social policy as part of design have been hindered by distant and clumsy bureaucracies. Designers have now realised that a higher level of individual empowerment and participation is required, but many present political systems seem biased against this. At Zaanstad, the design group hopes to establish a framework which will enable a variety of individual and partisan objectives to be satisfied within a whole that is greater than its parts.

The authors would like to thank: Robert Webb, Andrew Grant and Wyn Davies from Battle McCarthy; Tim Stonor and Mark David Major from the Space Syntax Laboratory at the Bartlett, UCL; and Alan Penn and Ruth Conroy from the Intelligent Architecture project at the Bartlett, UCL.

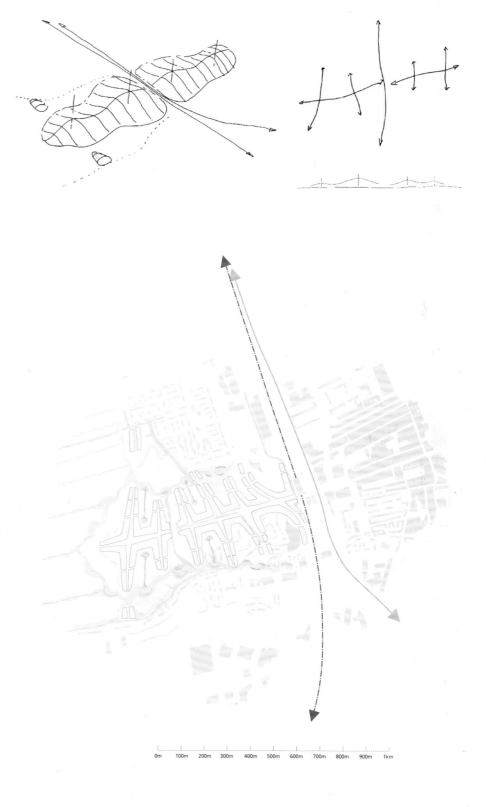

OPPOSITE: Potential massing; FROM ABOVE: Massing model; Development zones shaped by movement and landscape

A BREATH OF FRESH AIR

It has long been accepted that buildings can make people sick. Yet it may be that the real issue in the future is what buildings can do to make you well – by protecting occupants from the extremes of outside air quality. Most of the problems of ill buildings are now understood and can be avoided with good design. But the problem of air pollution – the atmosphere in which buildings dwell – is posing a threat from outside which is very difficult to master.

Many buildings designed and constructed today will suffer from increasing air quality problems in the future. If the siting, orientation or servicing strategy of the building exacerbates rather than improves the quality of air and affects occupant health, will it be the responsibility of the developer, the architect or the engineer?

Poisoned air

Over the past three years, a series of pollution peaks in world cities, mainly as a result of petrol and diesel fumes, has caused death and controversy. In May, June and July 1995 for example, ozone levels in European cities exceeded EU and World Health Organisation (WHO) limits in more than 2,800 cases, with high pollution levels being reported in 76 major cities. The results are not purely academic: 170 people died in London in November 1991 as a result of the smog, according to *New Scientist*. Meanwhile the world's ecosystems are suffering major damage, and certain species are facing extinction due to poor air quality.

The anatomy of atmospheric pollution

High pollution levels occur when it is very hot, or when it is very cold; when windless conditions or a temperature inversion allow ground-generated pollution to build up, and when hot sunlight causes pollutants to react in the air. The effects vary: ground-level ozone causes stinging eyes and breathing difficulties; carbon monoxide renders red blood cells useless; and particulates lodge in the lungs causing respiratory disease.

Not everyone is sensitive to environmental pollution, and those worst hit tend to be those with respiratory diseases or asthma. However the number of people who are sensitive seems to be increasing, as in the case of asthma.

More than three million people in the UK now suffer from asthma and nine million suffer from breathing problems, according to the National Asthma Campaign.

Design team response

Air pollution is just one issue among many – one source requiring design synthesis – and statistics are only partially useful without context. There is no doubt that London air is cleaner by far than in the days of coal, when as late as the 1950s not hundreds but thousands of people were dying each year in coal-smoke smog.

It is not a question of the presence of pollutants or poisons – which abound in nature – but in their concentration. Design teams can no longer design in ignorance of site air quality when the means of measurement are available at moderate cost and the links between poor air quality in buildings and poor health are generally accepted. Building design should now include the measurement of existing air quality from site surveys, historical data and medical records, and the establishment of guidelines for acceptable air quality related to exposure periods.

Sniffer buildings

Future buildings will be able to sniff the air around them before deciding which way to breathe. This will not mean the end of natural ventilation (air conditioning makes no difference to air quality and filtering can break large safe dust particles into small dangerous particles). It means an extension of building control intelligence to include air quality, and the development of different ways of dealing with the problem. Buildings may change inlet positions, switch to mechanical ventilation, or use electrostatic precipitation to remove particles. They will even use plants to purify and perfume the air in response to changing requirements (research by NASA has revealed how some plants can be used to absorb certain pollutants – for instance spider plants have an affinity for formaldehyde).

The important factor is that the list of critical environmental design issues: daylighting, acoustics, ventilation, thermal comfort, and the aromatic environment must now be extended to include air quality – at least until our transport systems can be revolutionised.

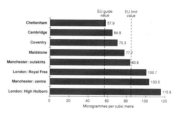

Levels of Nitrogen Dioxide in UK cities

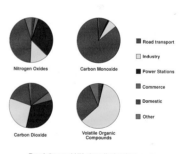

Breakdown of UK air pollution by source
Data from DoE for 1988

OPPOSITE, MAIN PICTURE: Police in protective clothing during the Tokyo gas attacks; FROM ABOVE: Designers are only as good as their ability to allow for future change; typical levels of nitrogen dioxide in UK cities exceed both EU guide levels and EU legal limits; the major cause of air pollution is road transport

The authors would like to thank Professor Patrick O'Sullivan and Robert Webb for their assistance in the preparation of this article

EMBODIED ENERGY

Give to the Earth and the Earth will give to you,
Take from the Earth and the Earth will take from you.
Traditional African proverb

'Recycle and reuse' exhort the bill boards of a new town somewhere along the Pacific Rim *circa* 2025. The city itself is angular and abstracted, the product of the rational decision making of town planners and urban engineers. Back in the old world charm of Amsterdam, city folk cycle to work through tree-lined avenues, past an eclectic mix of old and new. In energy terms, both cities are models of the new sustainable society, but what of the quality of life?

Renewing City Fabric

The fabric of our cities is the result of slow underlying change combined with bursts of development associated with external forces, either natural or man-made. This is an evolutionary pattern similar to that found in all natural systems. The Industrial Revolution, the Blitz and information technology all forced major changes to the city and its fabric. As we reach the millennium, man's awareness of our effect on the planet will change his approach to urban design once again. Significant ecological damage and global economic instability is being generated by our profligate use of energy resources in building, transportation and industry. Within this framework, construction is the largest source of pollution.

In the UK, there are over 20 million existing buildings in various states of health. The sickest buildings are rightly being demolished, but the majority, with careful surgery, can be maintained, refurbished and reused. This strategy will help reduce the pollution associated with demolition, reduce the consumption of embodied energy in new constructions, and, if the building's new skin and systems are designed with the environment in mind, minimise the daily use of energy throughout the structure's lifetime.

This design work will not be about preservation in aspic, but will make use of our latest understanding of materials, technology and work patterns. Urban renewal will take place at all scales: how the building fabric works; how the structure relates to its surroundings; and how people use the internal spaces.

Demolition or Revival

Demolition costs money and creates local environmental pollution through noise and airborne particles. The waste materials are more often than not dumped in ever-decreasing landfill sites, and their embodied energy is lost for ever. Designers often feel that the best solution to our clients' problems lies in new construction. Interestingly enough this option also provides them with the most freedom to express their creative energies and leave the greatest mark. But is it really the best solution? Can designers, with imagination and analysis, provide for their clients' needs through the revival of existing buildings? By reusing and modifying existing structures and ensuring that the buildings are fully utilised, it will be possible to improve the urban fabric whilst minimising our environmental impact.

This strategy is most relevant to our run-down inner cities, which are perfectly located for the new multi-centred multi-modal integrated conurbations of the future. These cities will be pedestrianised and serviced by highly efficient low-pollution public transport and telecommunications. Buildings will be designed to open on to the streets, be naturally ventilated and comfortable, yet still provide for the needs of a modern society.

Embodied Energy in Construction

At present, the embodied energy used in the construction of new structures represents 1020 per cent of the lifetime energy consumption of the building. With improved environmental design, this energy is certain to represent a higher proportion of the total.

The United Nations energy optimisation programme currently provide tables for minimising the embodied energy usage of building materials. Much of this energy exists in the structural frame of the building. Embodied energy audits can also be carried out to show the environmental value of refurbishment over demolition. The audit includes the energy contained in the materials, the energy needed to demolish the building and the energy required to rebuild it. A further audit could compare the lifetime energy requirements of the refurbished building with those of an environmentally sensitive new structure. This

OPPOSITE: Buildings are our most valuable possession, which is illustrated by this farmer transporting his house to a better location; FROM ABOVE: Trees grow and adapt, replacing their outer skin each year whilst retaining their basic structure; unlike nature, man often finds it easier to start afresh

analysis can even be extended to cover the requirements for transportation to green field sites, the work habits of the building users, and the nature of the work itself.

Comparative energy requirements of a selection of building materials:

Very High Energy	(GJ/tonne)
Aluminium	200-250
Plastics	50-100
Copper	100+
Stainless Steel	100+
High Energy	
Steel	300-60
Lead, Zinc	25+
Glass	12-25
Plasterboard	8-10
Medium Energy	
Lime	3-5
Clay Bricks and Tiles	2-7
Gypsum Plaster	1-4
Concrete:	
in situ	0.8-1.5
blocks	0.8-3.5
pre-cast	1.5-8
Sand Lime Bricks	0.8-1.2
Timber	0.1-5
Low Energy	
Sand, Aggregate	<0.5
Flyash, RHA, Volcanic Ash	<0.5
Soil	<0.5

One giga-joule of energy is the equivalent of one hundred days of food for an average man.

Energy Audit

Battle McCarthy is currently renovating a listed building in Soho, London. This office was built in 1913, is 8 storeys high and has an area of 3,500 square metres. Its masonry walls are up to 0.6 metres thick, the steelwork weighs 500 tonnes and the concrete slabs occupy 700 cubic metres. The embodied energy, mainly contained within the steel frame, equals 30,000 giga-joules; the equivalent of five personal computers running continuously for 1,000 years. Demolishing the building would add another 10 to 15 per cent to the energy usage, the waste material would fill two Olympic swimming-pools and the lorry would travel over 15,000 kilometres to and from a suitable landfill site. Realistically, a new building to replace the original might be built to more efficient environmental standards, and consume a further 20,000 giga-joules. The total embodied energy

would be sufficient to operate a naturally ventilated office for over 15 years.

Future Cities

If future cities are going to be sustainable, then all contemporary buildings will require refurbishment and renovation. Buildings which have deep plans, air-conditioning and poor illumination may be best replaced.

Many traditional buildings, especially those which incorporate narrow plans and exposed structure, can be renovated to meet higher environmental requirements. Rainscreen cladding, sophisticated window designs, new light wells and modern technology can be used to make them fit for a new millennium.

Modern buildings from the much maligned post-war era also have the potential to meet far more demanding environmental standards. Battle McCarthy's investigations into the refurbishment of the Martini Building, Brussels, illustrate that the incorporation of new facades, new plant and renewable energy sources – in the form of a roof-mounted wind turbine – can transform a poorly performing building into a racing thoroughbred. In a sluggish economy, the financial advantages of refurbishment cannot be ignored.

The exploration of how to reuse our infrastructure, for new patterns of work and relaxation, and in terms of the city ecology, will be exciting and fruitful, creating a fusion between new and old technology. The resulting buildings will not be simple renovations of the original architectural vision, but will be re-clad, shot through with communication technologies, and subtly re-engineered to allow for a natural flow of light and air.

Mathilde locked her bike and walked through the GOR-TEX curtain which wrapped around the north face of her company's 1950s headquarters. Light filtered through from a photovoltaic wall of glass to the south. In the lobby, her work-mates held trans-continental holographic conversations with an Indo-Australian client . . . it was a warm summer day but, a cool breeze from the basement heat sink gently ruffled the leaves of a tree fern.

The authors would like to thank Dan Philip and Douglas Broadley for their assistance with the preparation of this article.

OPPOSITE: The energy embodied in a typical small office building related to other basic needs for transport and food; FROM ABOVE: Daily we consume one million days' worth of stored solar energy as we burn coal, oil and gas to maintain our current lifestyles; an understanding of chemical interaction allows man to create catalysts to speed the manufacture of useful bio-materials – building designers now have the capacity to catalyse the usefulness of our cities through a greater understanding of the complex interactions of nature and society

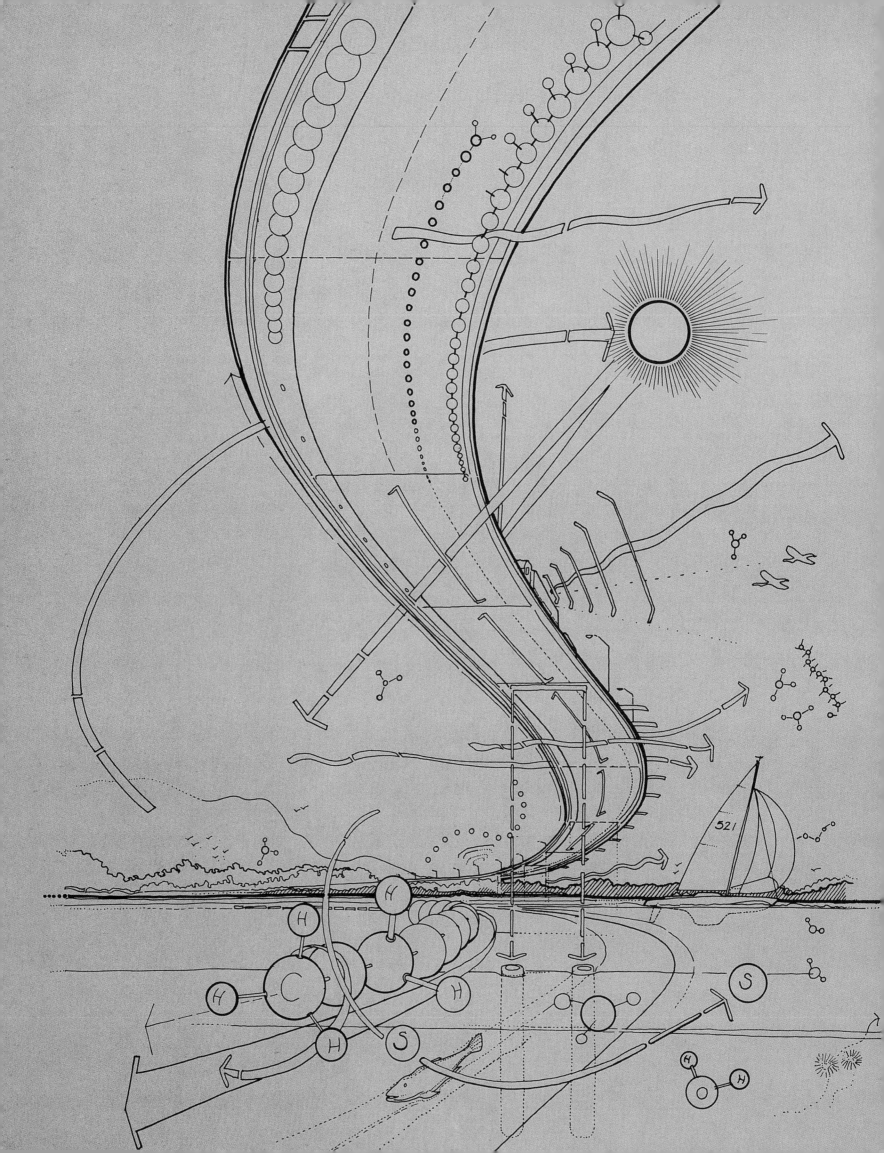

MORE FOR LESS

As the Millennium approaches, designers are conscious of three fundamental influences on the planning and design of new bridge structures: concern for the environment; innovation in technology and materials, and financial constraints. The Poole Harbour Bridge Competition presented an opportunity to reflect these issues and to provide a contemporary bridge design that is fully suited to its setting, aesthetically pleasing and cost-effective to construct and maintain. The elegance of the scheme lies in its double curved plan and its lightweight construction, which reflects its sensitivity to its internationally renowned environment.

The design of major structures is often dominated by consideration of one or two issues, such as structural form or cost. This scheme integrates a range of considerations into this process, and places environmental concerns alongside engineering and economy on the design agenda. The resulting structure is as much a response to local wildlife and archaeology as it is to structural performance criteria and the retention of shipping lanes. The use of the long gentle double curve is a consistent feature of British art, especially popular when used in landscape settings. As John Summerson stated in 1963: 'They possess an elegance and humanity derived to the° straight of the too embracing curve.' William Hogarth summed up the value of the double curve in his *Analysis of Beauty* in 1753 when he stated that: 'It leads the eye in a wanton kind of chase.' In addition, he recognised the need to find the optimum alignment: 'Though all sorts of waving lines are ornamental when properly applied: yet strictly speaking there is one precise line properly called the line of beauty.'

This preferred alignment, neither too curved nor too slight, is the basis of the design. Using this plan, the bridge becomes a dynamic part of the landscape and opens up new visual opportunities that would otherwise be missed by a simple, straight structure.

Journey as an experience
Modern motorway geometry often precludes, or denies, the potential for creating sculpture in the landscape. However, this double curve conforms to design standards and provides elegance to an otherwise very simple structure.

The alignment of the curves 'throws' the views from the bridge either outwards towards Poole Harbour and the wider world, or inwards towards Holes Bay. This complements the sense of leaving, or entering, the country, and creates a distinct split in the visual character of views gained in each direction: increasing the sense of natural intimacy to the north, and urban activity to the south. The double curve also allows the high point of the structure to coincide with the location of the navigation channel used by shipping.

The bridge
The road deck is supported on a simple 'goal post' structure and maintains a constant depth and profile. Visual interest is maintained through the variations in the bridge's height along its length. Similarly, the intention is to develop different qualities and spatial characteristics at either end of the bridge, further enhancing the environment and thus the visual sequence enjoyed from the bridge.

North landfall
Here, the various approach roads climb up new embankments to an elevated roundabout, giving dramatic views of the bridge and Holes Bay. To facilitate this the designers have maintained an open aspect in the area, with minimal tree planting. The land beneath the bridge will be developed as an esplanade to reinforce the current use by shore anglers and pedestrians. This hard urban structure will be softened by its close proximity to the rich grassland and heath.

South landfall
In contrast to the northern landfall, the southern approaches will not offer spectacular views of the bridge but will be surrounded with a soft woodland environment. The sense of enclosure, between the shoreline and the roundabout, will be reinforced with earth embankments.

The bridge gradually merges with the landscape in a gentle way, that blurs the distinction between Holes Bay and dry land. The landscape is designed to disguise the definition of the flood protection core and to create a seamless succession of natural environments: from open water to woodland.

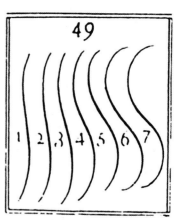
Hogarth, Lines of Beauty, *1753*

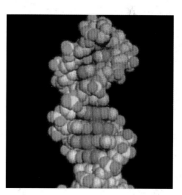
DNA spiral model, 1953

Natural/Urban interface

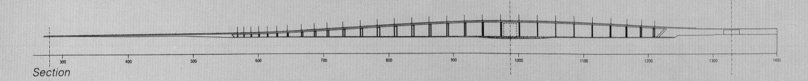

Section

Low level section

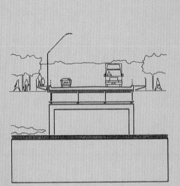

High level section

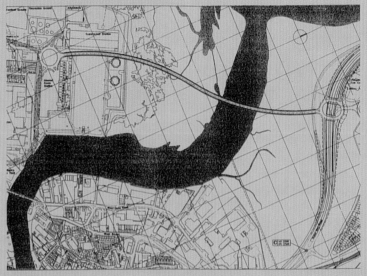

Site plan

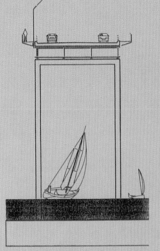

Main visual area

Regeneration & conservation

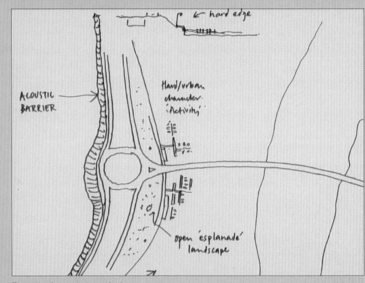

Detail of north landfall

Principal roosting areas

Recreational access

Land use

International context

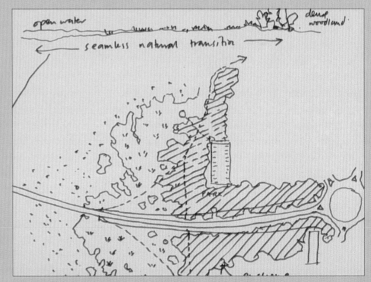

Detail of south landfall

This natural landscaping reflects the existing habitats while attempting to increase their scope. In addition, the scheme recognises the potential for the creation of a public park, in front of the old Poole Power Station site, to further reinforce the setting of the bridge. This strong woodland framework will also screen views of the remaining transformer buildings.

Structural efficiency

The structural objective is to get vehicles safely and efficiently across the bay, while allowing adequate space beneath for shipping. The proposed scheme provides the minimum structure necessary to meet these basic needs.

Structural economy

The proposals distribute the financial expenditure for maximum environmental and structural benefit. The intention is to show how the money is spent through the appearance of the scheme by minimising foundations and hidden structures.

Three material options have been considered for the bridge's superstructure: all steel; steel columns and deck with carbon fibre walkway, and all carbon fibre. An engineering value analysis – assessing cost, buildability, maintenance and durability – will determine the most appropriate solution.

The design team has also explored the possibility of incorporating intelligent systems within the primary structural elements. In this scenario state of the art sensors, such as fibre optics, would provide detailed on-line information about internal stress, strain, temperature and vibration. This information would be monitored by signal processors programmed to alter actuators – elements capable of altering their shape, stiffness, frequency and other mechanical characteristics – to counter the effects of structural deformation.

Ecology

This bridge responds to the ecology and landscape that occurs in the bay. The proposed landscaping is intended to build upon this natural foundation, creating an enriched environment for wildlife and people.

The method of construction and the design of components will be tailored towards the most energy efficient and environmentally acceptable methods. Applying the principles of ecosystem planning and management, the designers have adopted techniques that will minimise waste, avoid excessive use of energy, and prevent pollution of the environment.

The limited tidal range of Holes Bay – 1.8 metres approximately – precludes the use of barges and caissons and – despite the polluted nature of the mud and the tidal nature of the bay – most of the construction for the foundations and bridge piers will be carried out from causeways built on the mudflats. Once the foundations and piers have been constructed, these will be removed and the material reused in the construction of embankments and approach roads.

The authors wish to acknowledge the help of Douglas Broadley in the preparation of this article.

Project Team
Troughton McAslan
Architecture
Battle McCarthy
Environmental Engineering and Sustainable
Landscape Engineering
J M P
Structural, Highway, Civil, Marine Engineering and Project
Management
Davis Langdon and Everest
Costing
Dorset Ecological Consultancy
Local Ecology
Stephen Crute Associates
Environmental management
DNV
Noise and Air Quality
AC Archaeology
History and Archaeology
Wrigley Associates
Planning, Tourism and Leisure
JP Water Resources Consultancy
Hydrology

Sea aster in the salt marsh

Oystercatcher on the mud flat

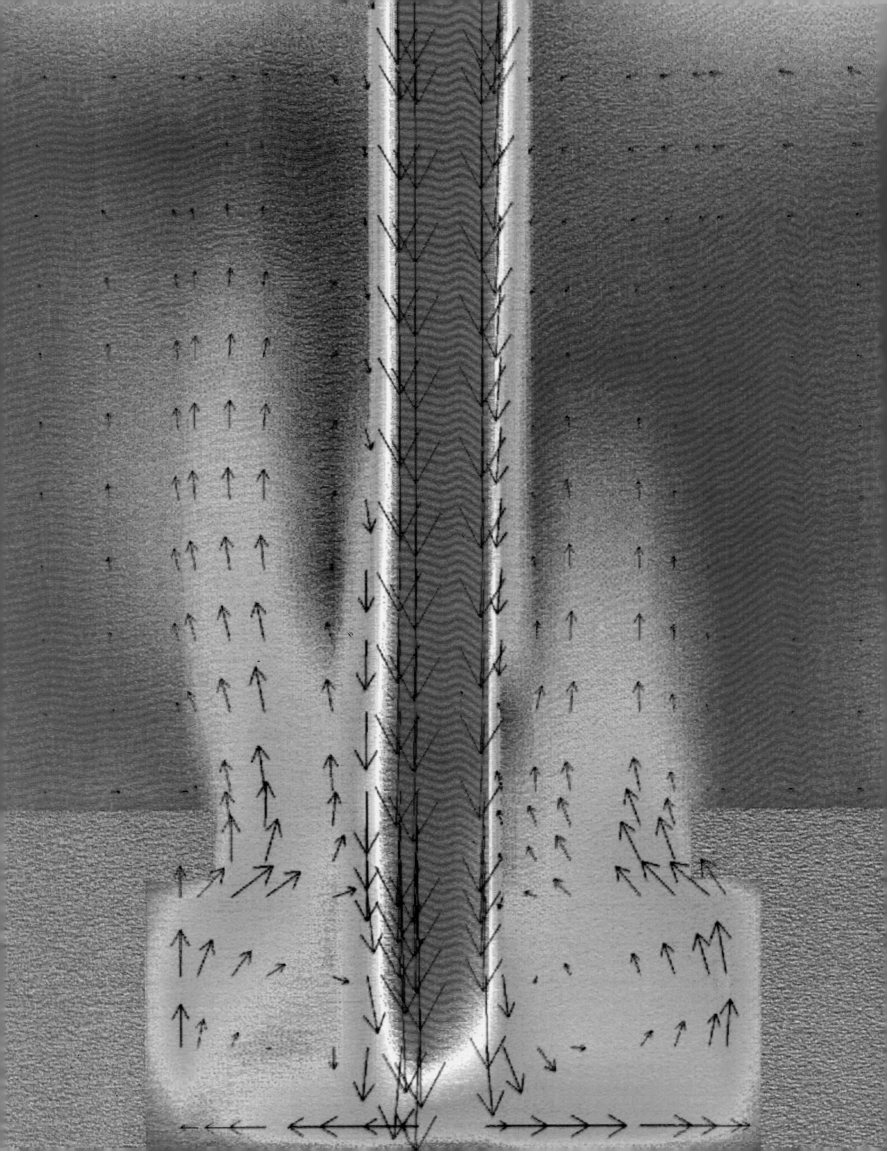

POST AIR-CONDITIONED ARCHITECTURE

'. . . all that man obtains by his own exertions . . . or from long use has become so important to human life that few, if any, whether from savageness, or poverty, or philosophy, ever attempt to do without it.'
Henry David Thoreau, *Walden* (1854)

Climatic forces are responsible for the shaping of a new generation of buildings. Architects are now designing structures which utilise the free energy available from the environment rather than simply erecting an environmental barrier and creating an artificial internal climate. The future architecture of the millennium has the ability to adapt traditional wind ventilation systems with ingenious building management methods to create low-energy, highly efficient structures. This new breed of building not only reduces running and maintenance costs and CO_2 emissions, it also enables the occupants to have more control over their environment.

In cold climates, wind has traditionally been seen as a negative force and buildings have been located and designed to minimise its effect. Increased occupancy and high internal gains due to office equipment have led to a greater reliance on air-conditioning, and with it the attendant cost and environmental implications. Architects and engineers are now considering traditional forms and devices developed in warmer regions and are successively translating them into what is rapidly becoming the new vernacular of post air-conditioned architecture.

Wind-driven ventilation finds its origin in historical precedents such as the wind towers of the Middle East, but it is also in evidence in the natural world. Termites are known to incorporate the basic principles of the stack ventilation system within their mounds. Termitaries are often shaped so as to have a greater exposure along the east–west axis so that the vertical passages inside the mound are heated by the sun. Warm air will then rise up through the passages and in turn pull cooled air through the damp soil at the base of the mound. Wind passing over the mound also contributes to the chimney effect as a negative pressure will draw air up through the passages.

Natural ventilation is achieved by utilising the inherent pressure differences surrounding the building caused by the wind and stack effects. The pressure differences between the inlet and the outlet locations provide the power to force the air through the building. Air movement within the building must also be considered in terms of buoyancy (thermal forces). Chimneys work because of the variation between the internal pressure at the top and the bottom. This is due to the different temperatures of the gases within and can be further enhanced by using the radiation of the sun on the chimney to act as a thermal stack. The general rule is to take in air low down and push it out high up as this is how buoyancy acts. It is therefore better for the wind to apply its force in the same direction as the buoyancy force to avoid a situation where the two cancel each other out.

Wind towers, wind scoops and solar wind chimneys are becoming a viable option for maximising the ambient low-grade energy resources of the North European climate. There is insufficient sunshine to rely on solar gain as an energy source and it is therefore necessary to look at ways of reducing the energy input into buildings. Air-conditioning contributes to a large percentage of the building's energy consumption and natural ventilation must therefore be measured as the principle environmental building issue.

Achieving a satisfactory system involves the development of an environmental strategy at the preliminary stage of design. A complex building in a complex environment means that the size and location of the inlets and outlets must be chosen with extreme care. There are of course certain cost implications in providing natural ventilation by means of wind towers. Internal floor to ceiling heights rise by up to 25 percent to allow for air movement, and the construction of the wind tower will increase the roofing costs. This, however, must be balanced with the reduced running expenses and the controllable climatic benefits to the user of being able to open a window and have direct access to the external environment.

ABOVE: By placing a building in the path of an air stream, a pressure differential will be set up. The molecules of air hitting a surface create a force and thus a pressure against the building. The wind speed having to pass over the building is increased and this will create a lower pressure on the leeward side of the building.(Photograph by Imperial College, London)

OPPOSITE: Computer fluid dynamic analysis of a wind scoop. (Image by Integrated Environmental solutions)

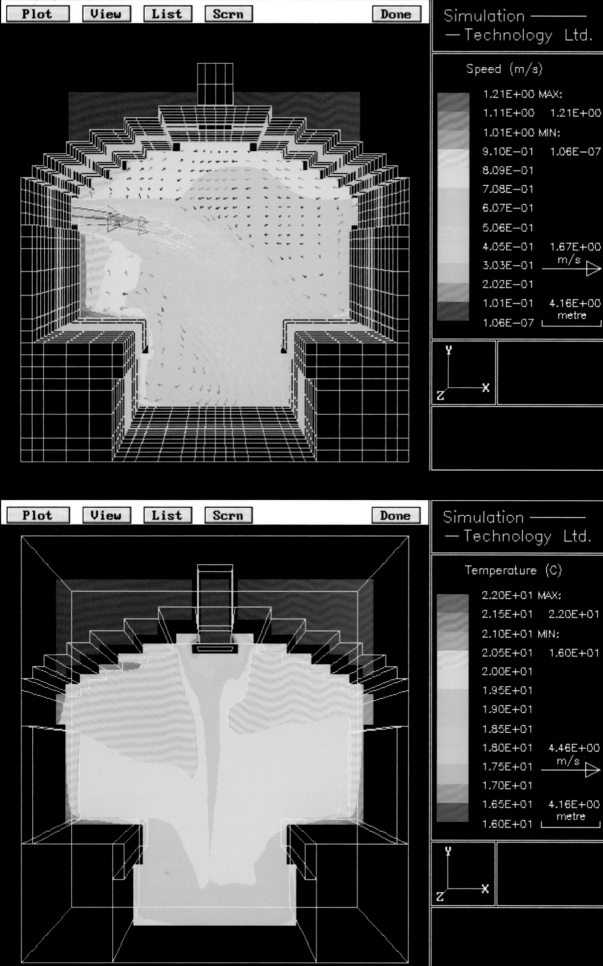

Wind Towers

The most efficient design for a wind tower, which will provide suction in all wind directions, is a vertical tower which projects above its surroundings and has an open top. If the ingress of rain is a problem, then a cover can be placed over the top so long as the wind is free to blow between the two. Air can be supplied through openable windows, allowing the occupants control of their environment. A central atrium with wind towers above ensures a constant flow of cross-ventilation and a high degree of controllability, even during high winds.

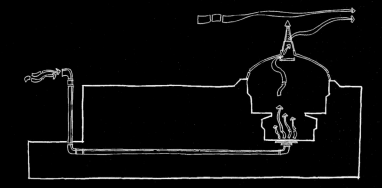

Wind Scoops

Wind scoops are a method of 'catching' the external airstream to provide fresh air to the building. They are particularly effective when supplying large open spaces such as atria, allowing cooler air to mix within the space. Supply air can be brought through fire escape corridors, enabling a breeze to flow horizontally through the building; but alternatively wind-scoops can be placed in the landscape some distance from the building and the supply air can be brought into the building via earth tubes. These utilise the steady soil temperature to provide free cooling in peak summer and, conversely, warming in summer. Wind scoops can also be mounted on roofs to allow cooler air to drop and mix within the space. Warm air is then extracted via the wind towers.

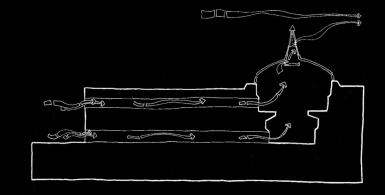

Mixed Mode Approach

To ensure comfort throughout the year a mixed-mode approach to ventilating the building is often taken. A naturally ventilated building can also incorporate an air-conditioning system. Natural ventilation, leading to major energy savings, is in use for the majority of the year, and the air-conditioning operated only during extreme summer conditions.

At present wind-driven ventilated buildings are few and have a minimum impact upon reducing the vast amount of energy that buildings consume. The new energy-saving building is, however, becoming a necessary reality and is developing a vocabulary of its own, at best celebrating its low energy virtues in bold and expressive forms.

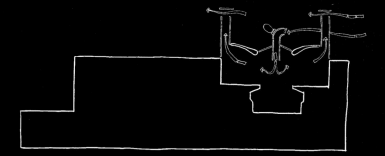

The authors wish to acknowledge Andrew Morrison's contribution to this article.

ABOVE: Three concept model designs to provide natural ventilation for a shopping centre.

OPPOSITE: Computer-fluid dynamic analysis of a wind scoop supplying fresh air to an atrium space. (Images courtesy of Simulation Technology Ltd)

WORKING WITH THE ELEMENTS

*Around the turn of the Millennium the . . .
population will change from being predominantly rural to being predominantly urban. This
compared with 14% urban dwellers at the end
of the 19th century, giving an indication of the
problems facing the infrastructure of the
present city. By the year 2000 it is predicted
that 22 cities will have a population of over 10
million, with three of these cites over 20 million.*
Statistics from the *Gaia Atlas of Cities*

A response to overcrowding in cities was first
apparent in the mid-twentieth century when the
transport revolution made it possible to develop
new towns and satellite cites within commuting
distance of urban centres. In Britain, in the
1950s, 13 new towns were developed. Many of
these later proved to be flawed as they had
been born on the drawing board rather than
evolving as a consequence of human needs
and site restraints. Ideological reasoning,
rather than a true understanding of the existing
ecology of the site or the consequences that a
new development would have for an area, often
dictated design issues. For example, Cumber-
nauld in Scotland was built on the summit of a
hill with the high street facing the direction of
the prevailing wind, producing considerably
more exposed conditions than traditional town
design. However, these new towns in Britain
became a model for planners all over the world,
with traditional building systems and devices
which responded to climate, ecology and 'way
of life' often being ejected.
   It is now clear that a new system of masterplanning is necessary if all the particular
parameters underlying the development of a
new town are to be understood. The designer
can then approach the problem from a pluralis-
tic point of view. A more suitable approach to
masterplanning is to understand the site on a
number of levels so that the town can be
designed to work positively with its natural

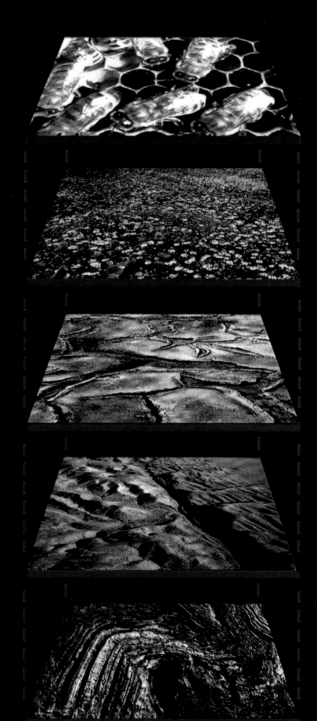

Form Finding: Layering

When addressing a brief it is important to have a thorough understanding of the site before conceptual and ideological concerns are considered. An engineering approach to masterplanning can give the site analysis an ecological basis. A matrix of analytical data can be created with a number of layers representing individual factors such as hydrology and topography. This method allows each to be clearly shown and easily understood. The combination of these layers can then point to the virtues of the site and its natural values can be enhanced. The layers are determined under the following headings, and organised to give a cross-sectional view of the site.

Fauna: By monitoring and recording the type and location of the wildlife of the region, the make-up of the natural habitat can be preserved. It is important to prevent a change in the ecosystem of the area as this can often have far-reaching consequences. Provision should be made for animals such as badgers and rabbits as well as hedgerow animals such as wood mice, shrews and voles. Existing waterways may contain fish, frogs and newts and the habitat of the local birds should also be addressed. One solution is to create a golf course within the new development, thereby creating a safe habitat for wildlife.

Flora: The species growing on the site and assessed for their visual and physical condition. Woodland, grasslands and hedgerows along with their relevant fauna should all be plotted to allow the designer to produce a landscape which is maintained by the existing ecology. Vegetation can provide a significant level of shelter and it is prudent to maintain the existing vegetation, not only for ecological reasons but because it reduces the cost of replanting and avoids having to wait for new vegetation to grow.

Hydrology: The water table and the natural watercourse across the site can have many implications for the form of the masterplan. Balancing ponds, for example, can ensure a manageable degree of irrigation, as well as acting as a reservoir for summer water supply. Canals between these ponds can also act as a water supply, produce attractive public spaces, and provide a means of transportation. Water is also a feature of innovative new environmental technology such as heat sinks and evaporative cooling. Waterways and ponds provide a natural habitat for many types of fish and wildlife, while fish farms provide an economic resource for the community.

Topography: The topography of the land is instrumental when planning the infrastructure and location of the residential/commercial areas and the landscaping. It should be developed to encourage passive environmental design. There are many advantages of positioning residential zones on south-facing slopes, including solar gains, protection from the cold north winds, natural irrigation, and allowing storm water to run off into the valley – where a country park could be located. The density of the housing should also be carefully planned: high-density housing should occupy the south-facing sites, whereas low-density housing can occupy north-facing sites, as a large plot allows the building to be rotated to face south.

Geology and Soils: The permeability and geology of an area also have a determining role in the positioning of elements throughout the site. It is preferable to build in areas with good drainage and avoid those where water erosion will occur. The clay content and base rock depth will all indicate preferable locations for the town.

This method of analysing the various eco-logical factors that make up the site gives an opportunity to design an infrastructure that works with the natural elements. This has many obvious advantages such as reducing infrastructure and running costs. It should also ensure that a policy of sustainability is adopted, though the success of this relies not only on the systems being set up but on the inhabitants understanding their implications.

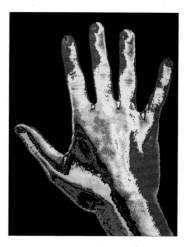

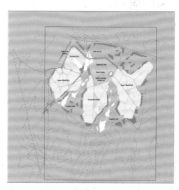

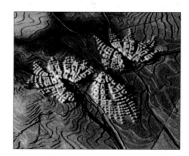

FROM ABOVE: Finger plans allow green belts to stretch into the centre of the town, between the 'fingers' of urban development; Cambourne masterplan, Terry Farrell and Partners; Parcbit, Majorca – topographic model, Richard Rogers Partnership

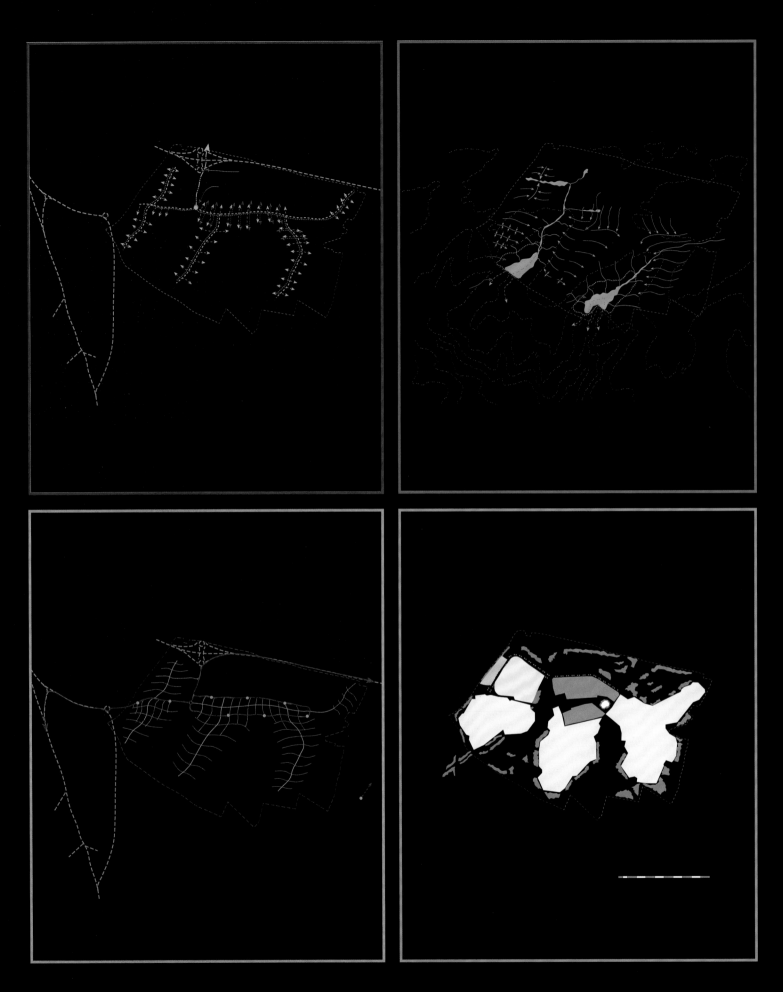

Interactive behaviour maps allow the designer to produce a policy of sustainability for a new town: red plan = energy; blue plan = water; orange plan = transport; green plan = landscape and ecology

Form Finding: Colour-Coded Behaviour Maps

The foundation of rural 'settlements' was based upon an assured food supply from the surrounding countryside. Limited by local restrictions, these settlements developed into towns and cities trading across the country and abroad. Trade and industry are now their backbone. With increasing urbanisation this has dangerous consequences: cities and many countries (for example, the United Kingdom) no longer produce enough food to feed their own populations, relying instead upon trade. To create a balance, a policy of sustainability should be adopted for every new town. Central design themes of sustainability are energy, water, transport, landscape and ecology.

Energy: A community settlement of approximately 15,000 will spend approximately £3 million per annum on energy for heating, cooling and lighting. This conventional design approach will result in the production of approximately 30,000 tones of carbon dioxide and 150,000 tones of sulphur. A sustainable energy strategy involves processes such as Combined Heat and Power, Energy Peak Looping or an Energy Power Generation Strategy. Fuel crops are already extensively used in Europe as an alternative energy source. Coppices are grown on a three-year rotation and harvested in January and February, allowing existing farm machinery and labour to be utilised.

Water: Water should be divided into two categories: fresh water (for drinking) and grey water (for use in bathrooms, etc). Reed bed filtration and sewage treatment are able to convert black water to grey water, providing a means of recycled water. Lakes can act as a form of water storage collecting ground water, which can also act as a heat sink to store energy and support a fish lake.

Transport: Non-vehicular forms of transport should be encouraged and bicycle lanes and paths provided. An efficient, broad-based public transport system can encourage a reduction in vehicular use, although it is impossible to avoid the fact that cars will always have a place in society. The car should not be discriminated against, instead creative traffic

planning should be adopted. This involves setting up control systems which alter, depending on the time of day or week and public holiday. These devices can constantly monitor vehicle flow and adjust it accordingly. They should not be seen purely as a means of reducing the weight of traffic, as traffic congestion on a high street can also be seen as a means of reducing speed.

Landscape and Ecology: Landscape should be given a useful purpose whether it is for producing crops, for nature conservation, climatic control or ornamentation. Productive areas can be allocated to grow fuel or food crops. It is also important to provide a suitable area of vegetation for wildlife. The landscaping of an area can also create changes to the microclimate, such as providing shelter belts.

It is the role of engineers to predict the effect that an action will have on our environment over time. Computer software has been developed that enables urban designers to do this. The computer can provide designers with a series of interactive behaviour maps associated with energy, water, transport and landscape/ecology for a particular site.

Spatial Analysis

The study of settlements shows that countries and, indeed, regions have developed different forms and hierarchies. These have evolved due to a wide range of perimeters from environment and climate, to security and society. There are therefore no universal rules for producing a good town design but the emphasis should be on producing an appropriate one.

An example of the danger of imposing unsuitable generic forms is the difference between British and continental settlements. Typical continental settlements are defensive in nature, either being walled or having a perimeter road. This provides an efficient means of distributing traffic as well as producing a feeling of enclosure. A typical English village, however, is linear in form with a high street running through it. The high street is particularly important in social terms and the 'ring road' form is unsuitable for providing the hierarchy that the linear form generates.

FROM ABOVE: Richmond, Yorkshire – informal plan with market street and 'fingers' of landscaping entering the town; Egushien, Alsace – defensive continental settlement where no green space is possible.

THE DESIGN OF SUSTAINABLE NEW TOWNS

By the 21st century 70 to 80 per cent of the world's population will live in concentrated urban centres. Nowhere is the demand for new towns going to be greater than in the developing world. As technology renders the field worker redundant and as population increases, more and more people will migrate away from their rural settlements to the urban centres, demanding housing, feeding, higher standards of living and thereby increasing pollution and placing greater demands on the world's already depleted natural resources.

To find the solution, we must first ask the right questions, for example, 'What are cities, how do they work?' Cities and towns are a complex mesh of people, lifestyles, machines, buildings, politics, power. However, from a purely engineering basis, they can be more simply defined as systems that import raw materials (input) to fuel a 'metabolism', that exports goods (output) and refuse material (waste).

This 'metabolism' can be fairly accurately defined in terms of input, useful output and waste, using a simple accounting and balance sheet. Typically a metabolic balance sheet would indicate that the actual useful product is small compared with the input (ie often less than 1%). Such studies also show the vast amount of waste that is typically put directly back into the biosphere (approximately 70%). In many cases, this goes back as raw pollution, leaving the biosphere to 'absorb' and process it for us. Following this philosophy, the earth can be viewed as a series of reservoirs (for resource) and sinks (for waste), both the reservoirs and sinks having finite capacity. At present rates the reservoir will quickly become empty and the sink full. It is therefore necessary to identify the various processes that go on to make up this metabolism so that their efficiencies can be improved, not only as individual cycles but also in the manner in which they can beneficially interact. There are two basic ways to view a city's metabolism. Either as a linear process, (input gives output plus waste) or as a cyclical process that produces feed back loops and recycles wastes. The key difference between these two viewpoints is that the linear system will eventually reach full capacity, whereas the circular system is sustainable.

The system can be identified by the following characteristics – *Linear*: water use high and is polluted; sewage is discarded; toxic fumes pollute; building materials and 'wastes'; trees felled without replacement. *Circular*: low water consumption, treated and recycled; wastes reused for fertiliser, heating and energy; fossil fuel used efficiently; building materials recycled and used discarded; trees replanted.

Any city can be designed (or evolve) from two starting points. That is the smallest module outward (ie building – streets – urban clusters – city, eg London) or from a strategic level inwards (macro planning, street scape, city blocks, buildings eg Manhattan). In most historic cases, this has been a process of evolution. London grew from a series of small clusters to become a massive urban conurbation, with the transportation and water systems being added as a result of growth (micro – macro). In contrast, Manhattan, grew from an initial orthogonal planning grid (macro – micro). But essentially both are the results of evolution rather than any real strategy, and thus the metabolism is generally linear rather than cyclical (eg refuse is rarely used to provide energy, it is merely transported out to sea and dumped as in the case of Manhattan). Indeed, both London and New York in comparison to many other 'mega' cities are extremely wasteful, producing 950 tonnes of rubbish per year per person compared to Mexico City which produces only 350 tonnes per person per year (a reflection on an affluent and effluent rich society!). However, within the developing world, with the ever increasing demand for new housing and new towns, neither approach has proved to produce an ideal result. The only real way to design sustainable cities is by being able to effect (ie design) both the macro and micro levels of the town simultaneously. For instance, it is no good designing an efficient energy production system if all buildings are going to be air conditioned and profligate energy users. Thus, it is absolutely essential that the designer (urban planner) has some means of regulating the amount of energy any building plot may use by legislation or guidelines. This does not mean that there would be a heavier handed planning approach, merely that there would be a more rigorous set of guidelines and targets for the designers to work to, encouraging them to

ABOVE: *Stockpile of cattle bones; Early inhabitants of the Galapagos Islands introduced horses as a means of transport, with little regard for the environmental consequences*

FROM ABOVE L TO R: Beehive; New York City;
Travelling Buddhist priest

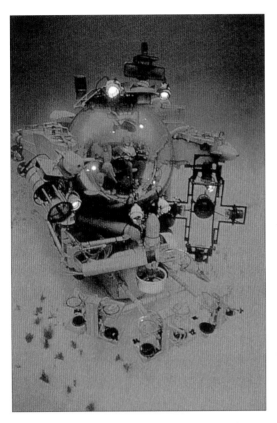

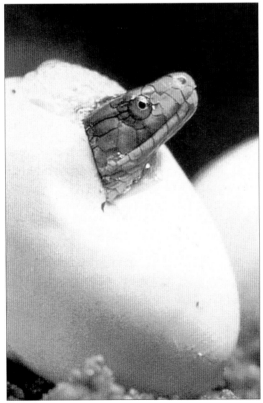

FROM ABOVE L TO R: Johnson Sea-link Submersible can descend to 1000m (3000 ft) from a surface support ship; Nutrient laden water supports plankton that feeds millions of fish; Snake hatching

maximise energy efficiency in return for floor area. Within existing cities, this is notoriously difficult to achieve. However, in the developing world, where new towns on green field sites are more common place, then such an approach is viable and essential for the well-being and balance of the earth.

A formula for sustainable development

A town's metabolism is comprised of six cycles which each have their own individual patterns but in some way all affect one another: transportation; energy; water; waste; micro climate, landscape and ecology; materials, construction and buildings. Naturally, many of the decisions to be made with respect to the above, are site specific and would necessarily take into account fundamental factors, such as: the climate (solar, temperature, humidity, precipitation, wind); geology (site conditions, materials resources, topology); location; economics of country, etc. However, in many cases the general objectives remain the same.

Sustainable transportation

This can be defined as transport which aids the mobility of one generation without compromising the mobility of future generations. Clearly many of today's transportation modes are not in keeping with this definition: the private car – the first choice of many in the developed world – is one of the major causes of the current high levels of pollution in our urban areas and in many places automobile accidents are the major cause of death in the under 50 age group.

Whilst the developed world is only now beginning to realise the irredeemable damage the car has done to society in terms of land-take, inner city deterioration, accident levels, air quality and noise, for the rapidly modernising and expanding economies of the developing world the problems are only just beginning. Rapidly increasing car ownership levels coupled with climatic humidity may soon mean that in many industrialising countries, environmental pollution indicators may soon exceed those currently being experienced in the industrialised nations. The challenge therefore is to prevent this foreseeable disaster from actually occurring without denying citizens of the developing world the indisputable benefits which increased personal mobility, facilitated by the car, can bring.

The key to a sustainable transportation system is the implementation of a transport hierarchy which gives priority to the pedestrian and public systems above the car. This does not necessarily imply positive discrimination against the private car: successful implementation of such a hierarchy can be achieved by merely creating an environment which does not cater for the car. This can be accomplished by limited

parking spaces, traffic calming, cheap mass transit and by establishing a network of roads unsuitable for vehicular traffic: pedestrian; cycle based; mass transit (public); car. The hierarchy chosen will dictate which modes have 'design' priority over others. Successful implementation of such a structure will depend upon a segregated environment and will fundamentally effect design decisions. The dominance of the car is based on its convenience. In order to encourage people to use public network and then walk (or cycle) it is important that the system must be of a high quality and provide similar or better service.

An acceptable walking distance within any town is about 150–300m or 5–10 mins maximum. Thus any mass transit system and urban plan should be based around this module. If walking is essential then pedestrian (and cycle) routes must be carefully planned to be scenic with good views; shaded from sun and passively cooled; streets narrow enough to provide shade; protection from rain; interaction with wild life and effect on the fauna.

There are two options for mass transit: high speed with large stop spacing (monorail) needing secondary modes such as taxis to cover intermediate distances; or slower speed (LRT, trolley bus) providing a comprehensive coverage to negate the need for other modes (except walking). Costs depend largely on the ground conditions and topography, however a broad cost comparison is as follows: Monorail $132m-$360m; LRT $48m-$162m; Trolley bus $19m-$25m.

Phasing is an essential element of any choice for it will effect timing and the magnitude of costs. One of the major perceived advantages of rail based (LRT) systems is this huge up front capital investment required, with no opportunity to accrue revenue until they are fully operational, despite the fact that environmentally and urbanistically they have great advantages. It is therefore essential to examine the possible phasing of such a system to achieve the same end goal: roads constructed for a bus system (Bio diesel); bus upgraded to 'trolley bus' (electricity produced from waste or CHP); profits used to fund rail infrastructure; light rail system (LRT) installed (clear electricity control over country roads can be pedestrianised).

Energy

Energy in the form of electricity, gas, oil is used within three broad categories: buildings 50%; transport 25%; industry 25%. The underlying principle of any energy strategy must be to firstly reduce the demand and secondly to provide the energy required from a renewable source thus creating a self sustaining (and in this case, even self sufficient) system. It is clear however that to achieve this, both the demand

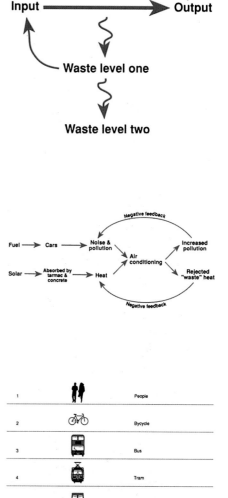

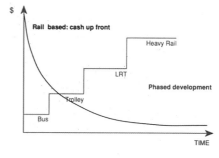

FROM ABOVE: Circular metabolism; Self-propagating use of air conditioning; Two methods of analysing the transportation hierarchy

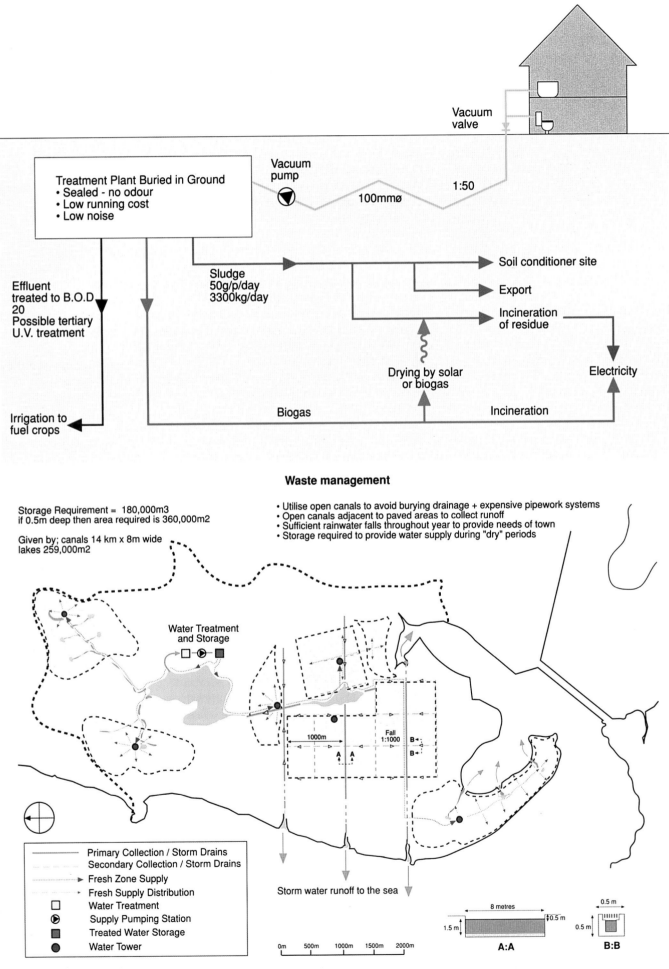

Vacuum valve

Treatment Plant Buried in Ground
• Sealed - no odour
• Low running cost
• Low noise

Vacuum pump

100mmø   1:50

Sludge
50g/p/day
3300kg/day

Soil conditioner site

Export

Incineration
of residue

Electricity

Effluent
treated to B.O.D
20
Possible tertiary
U.V. treatment

Drying by solar
or biogas

Irrigation to
fuel crops

Biogas   Incineration

Waste management

Storage Requirement = 180,000m3
if 0.5m deep then area required is 360,000m2

Given by; canals 14 km x 8m wide
lakes 259,000m2

• Utilise open canals to avoid burying drainage + expensive pipework systems
• Open canals adjacent to paved areas to collect runoff
• Sufficient rainwater falls throughout year to provide needs of town
• Storage required to provide water supply during "dry" periods

Water Treatment
and Storage

1000m   Fall
1:1000   B

A   A   B

Storm water runoff to the sea

———— Primary Collection / Storm Drains
- - - - Secondary Collection / Storm Drains
·····▸ Fresh Zone Supply
- ▹ Fresh Supply Distribution
☐ Water Treatment
◉ Supply Pumping Station
◼ Treated Water Storage
● Water Tower

0m   500m   1000m   1500m   2000m

8 metres   0.5 m
0.5 m
1.5 m   0.5 m
A:A   B:B

Water and waste management

92

and supply must be tackled simultaneously and by the same strategic design body.

Building demand can be limited by producing design guidelines and energy targets for given plots of land. Typically, this will influence decision making with respect to both the building systems and architectural response. Importantly, it will place greater emphasis on the architect to develop a building type that is environmentally responsive (or selective) rather than being environment rejecting. Thus buildings will need to be: naturally ventilated wherever feasible; daylit; limit use of air conditioning; utilise solar energy for heating, cooling and ventilation efficient systems; careful orientation and planning; appropriate materials choice. By adopting these principles, it may be possible to reduce the actual energy demand by up to 70%.

Energy is traditionally supplied in three forms, oil, gas and electricity. Both oil and gas used for heating, cooling, etc can only result in reduction in natural resources, and thus are *not* sustainable. Electricity, although traditionally produced by the combustion of oil, gas or coal, can be produced by the combustion or collection of renewable sources such as: incineration of waste or energy crop (Biomass); solar collection (photovoltaic or solar thermal); wind turbines. However, in all of these processes, the efficiency of the actual electricity production is less than 30%, the remainder being lost as heat (usually up a cooling tower). Essential to the achievement of a sustainable energy policy is the use of this 'waste' heat by the utilisation of combined heat and power plants (CHP). The heat can be used not only to provide winter heating and hot water but also (more importantly) as a source for driving absorption cooling machines. In this manner, the energy production process can achieve up to 85% efficiency.

Renewable sources include – *Biomass*: This includes plant materials that may be specifically grown for energy production (fuel crop) as well as organic wastes that will be generated on site. There has been significant progress with respect to the utilisation of energy crops for energy production. Such an approach has significant advantages in developing countries as they utilise local agricultural skills, low first cost implementation – quick to implement (1-2 years for first crop). *Solar energy*: Photovoltaic – utilises solar cells to convert direct sunlight into electricity (dc). They are fairly inefficient, (10–20%) and at the moment costly. *Solar thermal*: Uses solar energy to heat water to produce steam to drive a turbine etc. Used extensively in California – High capital costs, although they have great potential in sunny climates. *Winds*: Tried and tested systems. Their performance can be enhanced by integration into architectural building form. Following this philosophy, all

the new town would be all electric, with all heating, cooling, lighting, cooking, transportation and industrial systems (tram and/or electric cars) being based on electricity supply.

Water: In most countries, water is a valuable and scarce resource. It is thus important that a specific strategy is adapted that sets, as its prime objective, the achievement of a self-sufficient system; reduce demand; collect and store water over days or months to ensure that it is available all year round; treat and distribute water to areas of need efficiently; recycle waste water where possible for use in WCs or landscape. In any site specific area, it is necessary to carefully examine the precipitation and evaporation data. In many areas of the world, although there are long dry periods of little rainfall, there is often enough rainfall over the wet periods of the year to satisfy the yearly demand. However, essential to this strategy is an efficient collection and storage system. A typical balance for a new town development in a tropical climate indicates that enough rain falls through the 'wet' season to satisfy requirements during the dry season. In the example shown the town has been designed around the need to collect and store water in underground areas, tanks and lakes. The tanks form central squares and act as a significant thermal heat sink creating a cool micro climate within their immediate vicinity, whilst the above ground lakes and canals not only provide visual amenity but also a degree of evaporative cooling. In addition the canals from primary routes along which the landscape can be integrated to form pedestrian walkways and wildlife corridors.

Waste: Waste from a typical city can be broadly categorised into four forms: human effluent; bio-degradable/combustible waste (paper, vegetable materials); non-combustible waste (metals, glass etc); toxic waste. It is essential that the waste strategy is set to carefully deal with these four categories and that the 'waste' is not necessarily seen as something to be disposed of but as a resource to be recycled and re-used. Human effluent produces gas for heating/cooling/power, sludge for composting and water for landscaping. Biodegradable/ combustible waste can be cleanly combusted to provide power and heat, can provide compost and ash, can be used for road constuction/ aggregate. Non-combustible metals (metals, concrete, glass, etc) – can be recycled or sold on to other areas. Toxic waste must be reprocessed by specialist offsite plant. The simplest means of dealing with this is to ensure that all industrial processes are environmentally friendly and their waste can be easily dealt with.

Microclimate

The creation of a 'comfortable' urban micro-

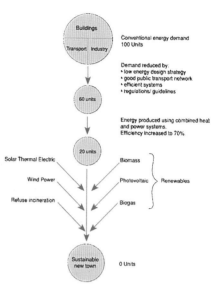

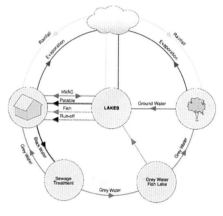

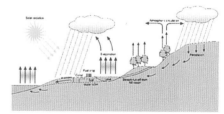

FROM ABOVE: New town energy strategy; Two methods of illustrating the natural water cycle; OPPOSITE FROM ABOVE: Waste management; Water and waste management

climate is essential to the successful operation of the urban transportation strategy of the new town. This will fundamentally affect the planning and layout of the urban environment. The response however will be site specific, primarily responding to the prevailing climate. The climatic elements within the urban area that can be modified by a sensitive urban design include: air temperature and humidities; radiant temperatures (surface) to which occupants are exposed; wind speeds in streets and around buildings; concentration of air pollution within traffic arteries; potential for natural ventilation; shading and potential for daylight; solar exposure and potential for solar energy utilisation. The urban factors that the urban designers have control over and that will effect these aspects are: topographical features of town; density (land cover) of buildings; distances between buildings; orientation and width of streets; urban parks, landscape; colour of buildings and streets; material choice (heavyweight versus lightweight). The aim of adopting such an approach is not to create an even level of comfort throughout the town, which would place too many restrictions on the design, but to create a changing thermal, air quality, acoustic and light 'topography' that recognises the need for varying landscapes. Thus streets may have a combination of fixed and variable shading systems. Bus stops and public squares may have a concentration of evaporative cooling systems (in hot/dry climates such as Seville) or permit good solar penetration (typical northern climate).Landscaping and green areas will play a vital role in the creation of the urbanscape and have a marked influence on the urban environment: provide outdoor shading, protection from cold winds; provide evaporative cooling; absorption of solar radiation; reduction in natural dust and air pollution particles; rainwater absorption; can impede or redirect wind to improve natural ventilation to buildings or surrounding areas. The landscape will also play a vital role in allowing fauna, flora and wildlife a natural path into and through the city. So that the town rather than merely destroying existing habitats can in some cases improve them or introduce new habitats and create opportunities for human and of wildlife interaction.

Materials
The choice of construction materials will play an important part in the sustainability of a new town. The primary objectives being that the materials should be: appropriate to the climate and the climatic response required; of local origin; low embodied energy; utilise local skills for construction; can be recycled; appropriate for the chosen structural regime.

In many cases, new towns comprise two to four storey developments. Although the use of steel or concrete is traditional for these buildings, there are many other alternatives, that in many cases can be sourced locally using local labour. *Stabilised soil blocks*: rammed earth; local soils, made locally; low cost and low embodied energy; can be used up to five or six storeys; recyclable. *Locally fired earth*: clay bricks; local skills; low cost; can be used up to five storeys. *Timber*: low cost, easy to use; sourced locally; replenishable source; low embodied energy; recyclable; *Fibre Concrete*: tiling (roofing); uses local materials (coconut and mud or cement). *Risk Hush Ash* (RHA); used to manufacture cement; burnt to provide energy and ash (100 tonnes rice = 5 tonnes ash).

Design Strategy
The very nature of this approach means that at first, each of these cycles should be analysed independently of each other and the urban plan in order to idealise their operation. It is then possible to create a multilayered design which is made up of all the individual components including the urban objectives. They can then be moulded together to create a working metabolism. This design process will involve highlighting the areas of both positive and negative interaction, leading to an emphasis of certain areas, that will inform the urban and architectural design. Thus, the plan for water may highlight a need for open lakes or canals, which can then be utilised as part of the landscape plan, and form an important element of the urban streetscape. Or the transport requirements for drop off points every 300m could form a module upon which the urban centres are clustered, which in turn may tie in with the requirement for water storage, etc.

In this manner, the urban planner, the architect and the engineers can work together with the various specialists to create an integrated plan and strategy based upon informed decision making. This approach to urban design is, however, more involved and more complex than the traditional methodologies for it involves examining the problem in not merely two or three dimensions, but in seven or eight dimensions. All towns and cities have metabolisms, that ultimately form part of the global eco-system. These metabolic cycles must respond to the demands for increased efficiency interaction so that they become sustainable Urban Environmental Design separates, idealises and then recombines these component cycles of the metabolism creating an environment and ecological topography that better satisfies todays demands for cleaner and better cities – *Towards a sustainable future*.

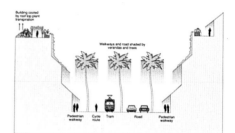

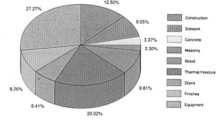

FROM ABOVE: Microclimate; Typical embodied energy in housing; OPPOSITE FROM ABOVE: Autonomous Living Capsule; Kayangez Atoll, Palau Pacific Ocean.

Thanks to: The Ngiom Partnership; Energy for Sustainable Development; University of London, Centre for Sustainable Development, The Martin Centre, Cambridge

INTERACTIVE URBANISM

Singapore's new city Nah-Sing was first conceived in 2010 and all major infrastructure completed seven years later. It houses 10 million people and the city design incorporates energy and food production so that there is an overall surplus of energy, fed to the grid to feed the antique towns of the last century. Its designers remain unnamed, though databases record that they numbered 2,372,981. They mainly lived in Singapore, though contributions were also made from California and a group working from Weybridge in the UK. The systemic simulation at the core of the design process modelled city development over a 200 year period, and predicted an ideal decommission time of 137 years. The city's worldwide fame derives from the swathes of forest penetrating its plan, and the vibrant ecosystems that the forest sustains; an idea that is thought to have originated from the Weybridge group . . .

'The experts are all saying that our big cities have become ungovernable. What the hell do the experts know?'
Richard Daley, Mayor of Chicago, 1902-1976

Avant-garde technical revelations have projected our industry in leaps and bounds in a shroud of technical secrecy and public scepticism. We are notorious for the lack of unanimity this inspires between public and professionals. The public representatives are baffled by our need for change, and we are exasperated by the conservatism of bureaucrats who supposedly represent the views and interests of the public.

Over the last decade or more, the balance of power has shifted to the public from our profession still apologetic about the mistakes of 60s' master planning. Unfortunately our professionalism is too often described as arrogant, self-interested, and elitist. However we should take every possible route to reconcile directly with the public rather than through their agents. For example, technical progress may evolve by igniting the community's artistic and technical interest and abilities on a mass Utopian scale through the use of the new communication highways. Public participation would then utilise the complete creative spectrum of our industry as we attempt to solve the mystery of our built environment, in unison not in isolation.

If you were told that 5,000 people were killed travelling by air in the UK alone last year, you would seriously consider ever flying again. However, although 5,000 people were killed on the roads last year, that knowledge is unlikely to keep you from using your car. The reason is that we accept more risk if we are personally involved with decisions than if someone else is responsible – in other words, the acceptable concept of risk is relative to the level of personal involvement.

Architects and engineers are constantly urging the public to take risks and support innovation in the constant search for new solutions to old problems. Given the scale of the social and environmental problems now facing us, it would be difficult to deny that fearless innovation was necessary. Yet are we approaching the community with innovation in the wrong way? To even begin to deal with the environmental crisis, humanity needs to be decisive about technology and the design of the human environment. The necessary changes may seem outlandish and strange – and by taking them, we risk losing the familiarity and perceived utility of the status quo. Inertia sets in, and problems pile up unattended.

The only way to achieve a sustainable future is to involve the public in the design and decision-making process, in the most fundamental way. We need to make people more familiar with the macro-environmental and social issues which planners and architects and engineers face; invite them to make proposals and suggestions for change, and allow them to explore the consequences of their ideas. If the challenges and problems could be understood in this way then everyone could participate, sharing responsibility for urban policy and environmental change. Real innovation would become inevitable as we all progress together.

If this sounds unfeasible, it is only because we are not yet familiar with the tools necessary to facilitate this process. Most current public participation exercises are deeply unsatisfactory. To enable a radically different process, radically different tools are required; tools are now coming into existence in the shape of the computer programs SimCity, SimTower and

OPPOSITE: Boxer – urban design is presented as a fait accompli *but its impact can not be underestimated; FROM ABOVE: Thermal satellite image of Merseyside – advanced information and image processing guides our new perception of human dwelling patterns; detail of St Helier, Jersey computer model – the simulated city is vibrant with industrial and commercial activities; babies – human interaction and communication provides a reason to live*

SimEarth, written by the software house Maxis. The programs are the starting point for an entirely unpredicted approach in design; the first of a whole new generation of computer programs, giving a tantalising hint of future possibilities for architecture, urban design and many other fields.

Maxis

The co-founder and chief programmer for Maxis, Will Wright, is a self-taught Apple and Commodore programmer, driven by his fascination with statistics. He has brought sophisticated techniques such as simulation and adaptive computing to personal computer users in the form of a new generation of entertainment and learning software. Maxis' 'software toys' are so successful because of the programs' ability to make artificial life and simulation technologies accessible and entertaining. Individual components in the simulation follow simple rules, yet when combined with other components, exhibit complex processes that closely mirror real performance. Dynamic simulative computing thus becomes faster and more accessible, operating on ordinary personal computers (which are themselves constantly increasing in specification).

SimEarth, SimCity and SimTower are living simulation programs for desk-top computers, which enhance learning through visual exploration, experimentation and creativity with time. The simulations make learning enjoyable, because they develop ideas by trial and error. The user may create and instantly see the consequences of ideas; developments which may take hundreds or thousands of years on a global scale, decades on an urban scale and years on a building scale.

SimCity

SimCity provides an overview of the city in development, displaying a 3-D animated model in vivid colours. The user can 'zoom' in and out from an overview to close-up, make changes to street layouts or land-use patterns and watch the results. With only one finger the user can demolish buildings, draw new roads, change tax levels and build sewage plants, power stations and industrial areas.

In effect, the user becomes city designer and mayor, taking control of a city's construction and maintenance and assuming responsibility for everything from building energy management, air quality enforcement, tax collection and the encouragement of economic and social growth. Based on the designer's decisions, and governed by a set of complex algorithms, the city lives and grows, or decays and collapses. For instance, if pollution is too great, transport provision inadequate, or energy production

insufficient, then the city will not thrive. Month-by-month and year-by-year, SimCity updates the conditions of economy, society and city fabric in response to the prevailing conditions, providing a directly visual dynamic analysis which allows designers to look into, and speculate about, future developments.

SimCity is an excellent tool for learning and exploration, based on a process of trial and error with the reward, when proposals are successful, of watching the simulated city thrive. If taken a step further, the models can also be adapted to represent real cities, both existing and proposed. Major cities around the world, including London and Berlin, are presently being modelled, and Battle McCarthy is already using the program as a design tool on large-scale urban developments.

SimTower

SimTower, still under development by Maxis, involves a parallel process on a different scale, where the user becomes the architect, engineer and quantity surveyor for a building. Each change to the building's design in progress has impact on the energy consumption, budget, floor area and success of the building; changes which allow the designer to learn by trial and error, and create a resonant combination of factors. SimTower will help the user to develop an excellent understanding of the process of building design, and with algorithms based on real data should provide an essential sketch design tool for architects and engineers. SimTower will also be placeable within SimCity, extending even further the modelling and learning possibilities of the system.

SimEarth

SimEarth is nothing less than its name suggests – a planet simulation. Its basic premise is taken from James Lovelock's GAIA hypothesis, the classic theory suggesting that elements of the planet form a complex system which, seen from above, seems to be responsive and even self-regulating. SimEarth treats the planet as a complex system of the following interacting factors:

Chemical: atmospheric, composition and energy management
Geological: climate, continental drift, earthquakes
Biological: formation of life, form, evolution, food supply, biome types and distribution
Human: wars, civilisations, technology, waste control, pollution, food supply, energy supply.

The user's objective is to manage the earth by making use of the available data in the form of maps and graphics. The software constantly performs checks, calculations and updated testing of your plans and theories as you watch

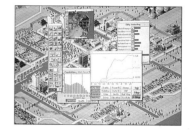

OPPOSITE: Boy swinging – assured balance and cooperaton are essential as we reach for the future and cross the void into new hope: FROM ABOVE: Slums, Caracas; detail of Jerai International Park computer model showing data sheets; high street UK – the slums of Caracas, Venezuela and the high streets of Britain, data analysis and interactive simulation via modem enables the occupants of both to become part of the planning process and contribute to each others' well-being

the earth develop or decline. Of course, a truly accurate simulation of the climate has yet to be achieved by the most powerful super computers operated by the leading Met Offices of the world, and the accuracy of climate models will always be limited by the chaotic nature of fluid systems. SimEarth nevertheless provides an exploration of the basic principles and the opportunity to visualise possible outcomes of change. As a learning tool, whether to explore James Lovelock's GAIA hypothesis or the dynamic of atmospheric change, it is invaluable. And it does not require a leap of faith to imagine a SimEarth scenario consisting of cities modelled, designed and developed in SimCity and allowing the consideration of global trade along with the energy and resource balance.

Interactive Urbanism

Using these programs, anyone will soon be able to propose a building, place it in a city and observe the city's global impact, all in a day's work. And if that is the case, then that person is immediately empowered to take part in the design and decision-making process, allowing in its turn the re-definition of associated risk, and enabling the innovative and comprehensive planning of the worldwide changes necessary to combat the crises of environment and population growth.

A number of themes arise from the Maxis programs, as design aids to the community in their pursuit of improving the built environment: (i) coordination and interrelation – the programs provide a means of integrating policy and investment, decision making to the complex and interrelated economic development, social policy (the reinforcement of social and economic cohesion), transportation and environment. (ii) shared responsibility and participation – the programs encourage the acceptance of responsibility for the consequences of our action at all levels of the individual, the company and public administration, which is a fundamental prerequisite for environmental improvement. They emphasise the need for an understanding and knowledge of these consequences which are often so lacking, yet remind us that an informed choice does not discharge us from our responsibilities. (iii) long-term objectives – the programs provide us with an insight into the future. They encourage long-term objectives well beyond the life span of the designer and work in favour of an attitude to using today's resources, which does not reduce their potential for future generations – the definition of sustainable development.

Pilot Projects

SimCity has sold over a million copies worldwide and is being used as child's game and for school projects. Battle McCarthy has been

pioneering its use in assisting in the design development of a number of major urban design projects such as Jerai International Park in Malaysia, and Palma New Town. As well as these new town and city projects, an island project has just started with Jersey Energy in the Channel Islands. This project first focused on the proposed 2 km^2 Water Front development which is to be constructed on reclaimed land adjacent to St Helier's harbour. The objective of the Island Project is to first involve the local participation for the design strategy for:

1	-	waterfront
2	-	harbour
3	-	town centre
4	-	parish of St Helier
5	-	all 12 parishes of the island

The first step is to install computers and touch screen displays at a number of public locations (the 'touch screen' facility makes it simple for people to interact with the computer, without worrying about mice or tablets – interfaces which not everyone is familiar with). Two versions of the St Helier model are provided showing the waterfront site with the proposed development and with a blank site. The public can therefore either amend the proposed scheme or propose their own ideas and see the consequences of their proposal take effect in front of them. Each proposal is recorded and sent back to a central design office for review. At the end of a two-week period, with the minimal investment of a few computers placed in public places, the design team has secured thousands of design ideas, and the people of the town have been given an enjoyable and entertaining opportunity to make a real contribution to the debate.

In stage two of the project, when the SimCity model is extended to the whole of the island, it will become a tool for the control of the environmental impact on the island. Because of commercial as well as environmental concerns, the local electricity company, Jersey Electricity, wants to avoid future expansion of power supply, but to maximise the return of the existing investment. SimCity provides an effective way of engaging public support and proposals on energy strategies for the island.

The island model, accessible from every Jersey household by modem, will enable users on Jersey to explore the parameters of domestic energy consumption, transport and power generation within a realistic model based on real data. Users will learn and understand about the importance of domestic energy-saving techniques and have the opportunity to explore, for instance, whether windfarms are a reasonable proposal in particular sites; along with other strategies for the island. Parishes and schools

The village of Secoton, painted by John White, 1585-93 – lively interaction of people and the managed environment

100

will compete with each other for prizes; the challenge being to come up with the most environmentally sound and cost-effective energy proposal for Jersey.

Conclusions

Give a man a short-term lease on a garden, he will make it into a desert.
Give a long-term lease on a rock and he will make it into a garden.
To create a sustainable future, the working of the whole system must be considered, not just the separated parts: planet; continent; country; region; town. District neighbourhood and building must be considered at once. They must also be considered as dynamic systems over time, as we know that simple systems can quickly generate complex and chaotic behaviour. Computer programs such as SimEarth, SimCity and SimTower are simple, accessible and affordable tools which will revolutionise the design approach towards our built environment.

It is fundamental that invention becomes the mainstream of our culture if we are to find solutions to the growing problems which face us. These programs will allow people to understand and participate in the design and decision-making process, enlisting their support for necessary innovation. They exploit the opportunity of collective decision-making based on qualitative judgements and allow the exchange of information which yields the unexpected, even unsought answers from which true innovation results. By involving people in the processes of designing the future the programs give people a reason to live.

For the immediate future such initiatives will be complementary to the design process rather than replace it; the computer models are obviously simplifications, as are all models, and therein lies much of their utility. Nevertheless, with the continuing spread of information superhighways across the world and the developing subtlety of the programs, ever greater possibilities will open up, and the role of architects and engineers will continue to change. Mass communication using sophisticated tools like SimCity could create a new era of scientific, organisational, social and intellectual creativity.

The city's worldwide fame derives from the swathes of forest penetrating its plan, and the vibrant ecosystems that the forest sustains; an idea that is thought to have originated from the Weybridge group . . . though no one can be sure of this. For the individuals connected together on the net became as neurons in a brain; acting in response to each other in a complex and unpredictable process. Ideas fired from site to site, gaining or losing momentum and always modified and influenced by the interaction with other aspects of the developing masterplan . . . The design process took 12 months, though most designers did not remain connected for more than a month, moving on to other tasks as their interests and skills waxed and waned . . .

The authors would like to acknowledge the contribution made by Robert Webb to the preparation of this article.

FROM ABOVE: Computer model of St Helier, Jersey, used in interactive planning exerise; Franz Kline in his studio – 'his pictures give the sense of too much pressure straining against too little space'; computer model of Jerai International Park, Malaysia – SimCity can empower the individual to understand and manipulate the urban environment

SCULPTING WITH ENERGY

The engineer's brief is to maximise the use of energy, materials and skill for the benefit of all. And yet most of the engineering that goes into the creation of our built environment is carried out too late. It is the strategic decisions, made in the early design process, that have the greatest influence on the environmental efficiency and success of urban proposals. Precise and cogent engineering analysis of a full range of strategic options is essential for use by everyone who is instrumental in shaping the built environment.

Rapid and simple analysis tools are needed to assess the implications of proposals at an early stage; and they need to be fast enough to allow multiple iteration, allowing a large number of options to be considered. In the early stages of designing a building, decisions on massing and orientation can have considerable influence on the eventual energy consumption of the building. Although later design decisions will also have an effect, it is important for the architect and client to be able to consider this aspect right at the start of the design process. Here we present the initial analysis that we have carried out on two projects, one in London and one in Hong Kong, which in their very different qualities reflect the differences of climate and urban density in the two cities.

Responsive Energy Modelling in London
This project, with Terry Farrell and Company, demonstrates the use of an amended version of the Lighting and Thermal Method, first developed by Cambridge Architectural Research, for energy massing analysis. When linked to a spreadsheet, used with a desk top computer modelling program, the method provides a rapid comparative assessment of a range of proposals.

The Method works by calculating energy consumption figures from different zones of a building, based upon the following factors:
- Local climatic conditions
- Orientation of facades
- Area and type of glazing
- Overshadowing from adjacent buildings
- The inclusion of atria
- Occupancy and vacation patterns
- Lighting levels
- Internal heat gains

The energy consumption and carbon dioxide emissions figures produced represent good practice, though they are not absolute, for it is impossible to predict actual occupancy patterns. Their primary value is to provide a comparison between different building options.

The objective of the computer energy modelling was not to lead the masterplan but gauge the potential energy consumption of each massing option. The first option filled the whole site with building form. As would be expected, this generated the highest energy demand as it requires artificial lighting, mechanical ventilation and cooling in all areas for most of the year. Fragmenting the building to 40 x 40 metre blocks did not reduce the energy demands by a significant amount as they were too deep to naturally ventilate and had poor daylight penetration. Thinner 12 to 15 metre wide buildings with the main facades on a south-north orientation, with atria and pre-heat to ventilation, generated the lowest energy demands due to increased daylight potential and the ability to use mixed-mode systems with natural ventilation in the mid-season condition.

Energy and the Community in Hong Kong
Frei Otto and Buckminster Fuller both speculated about cities in bubbles, as 'seen in their proposals for Arctic City and for Manhattan. While the concept of entire cities in artificial environments is likely to be undesirable, the principle has yet to be applied fully to buildings. In Hong Kong – due to the massive expansion of retail service requirements – podium levels are rising every year, to the point where they may eventually submerge the existing skyscrapers. In response to this condition, we have developed an advanced eco-tower proposal for the Hong Kong community with Terry Farrell and Company. The proposal consists of a single one-kilometre tower generated from a radical arrangement of buildings. The axial and stability loads are carried by the peripheral service core, which also act as collectors for solar power. Between the cores an active facade system controls the quantity of light and heat energy allowed into the development, creating a controlled environment within the buffer spaces.

Hot air balloon above the Alps

The scale of the proposal enables the tower to create an acceptable artificial 'external' environment using ambient energy sources such as wind, solar radiation, and pressure and temperature differences with height. The radial arrangement of the blocks creates an artificial enclosure with a maximum number of building facades shaded from direct sun at any time; the height of the building enables it to take advantage of the dramatic variations in climatic conditions over its height – including a six degree temperature variation – to drive a high-pressure stack providing ventilation. The surface of the cores and active facade are able to absorb a maximum amount of solar energy via photovoltaics. Thus the desired artificial climate is generated within which the offices operate, and they may be naturally ventilated throughout the year.

Further analysis will involve looking at the building layout to optimise solar shading and daylight penetration, and analysing the shape of the entire envelope; while a cylinder creates maximum volume with minimum surface area, a particular orientation of ellipse may provide a better response to the sun path.

Futures

With the new release of Sim Tower, the follow-up to SimCity by Maxis, we are provided with a basic tool to commence a conversation with the Hong Kong community about towers fo this nature, providing an understanding of the driving forces behind such a proposal, and what the tower might be like to live and work in. The tower design will thus become an example of the use of the full range of new engineering design tools.

The authors would like to thank Robert Webb for his assistance in the preparation of this article. The discussion of tower design is continued in the next issue of Architectural Design, *which focuses on the skyscraper.*

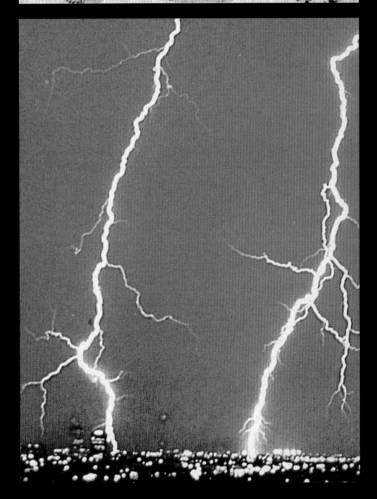

FROM ABOVE: Vertical axis wind turbine; lightning strikes above the city

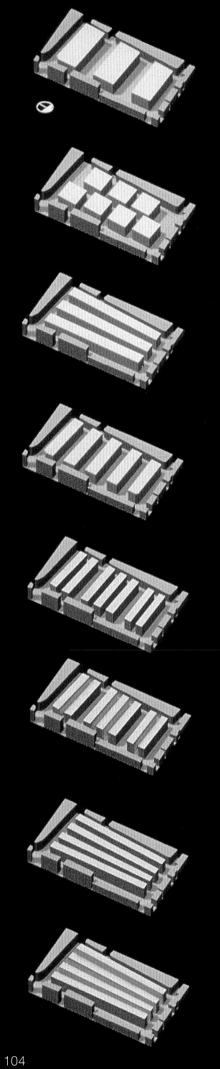

Energy Use 642 kWh/m^2

Lighting   Heating   Ventilation and Cooling

Carbon Dioxide Emissions 411 kg/m^{2}yr

Energy Use 634 kWh/m^2

Carbon Dioxide Emissions 393 kg/m^{2}yr

Energy Use 607 kWh/m^2

Carbon Dioxide Emissions 312 kg/m^{2}yr

Energy Use 650 kWh/m^2

Carbon Dioxide Emissions 327 kg/m^{2}yr

Energy Use 220 kWh/m^2

Carbon Dioxide Emissions 89 kg/m^{2}yr

Energy Use 112 kWh/m^2

Carbon Dioxide Emissions 65 kg/m^{2}yr

Energy Use 245 kWh/m^2

Carbon Dioxide Emissions 99 kg/m^{2}yr

Energy Use 124 kWh/m^2

Carbon Dioxide Emissions 88 kg/m^{2}yr

*Energy massing studies for a
central London site, showing
option tested and resulting
energy and carbon dioxide
emissions. The sixth and the
eighth options have atria used
as ventilation pre-heat;
OPPOSITE, FROM ABOVE:
Visualisation of daylight penetration and mid-season ventilation
in the resulting scheme: Atria act
to bring daylight into the building
and, utilising a wind-driven stack
effect, draw warm exhaust
air out of the building*

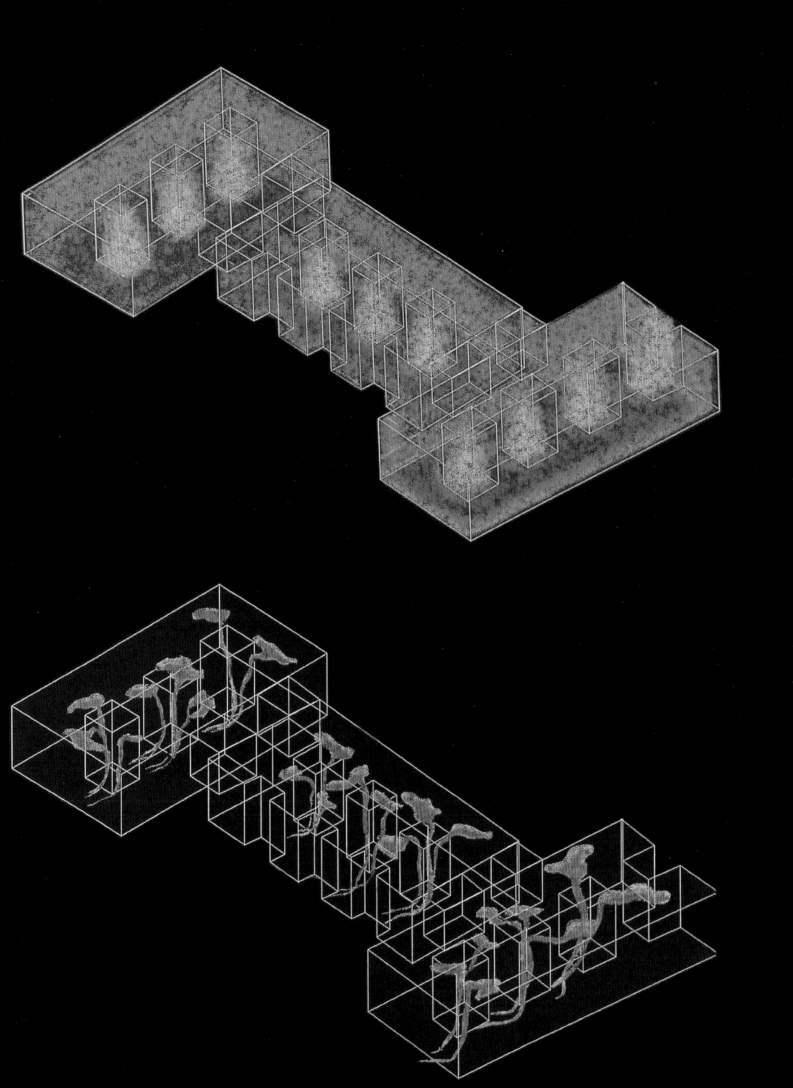

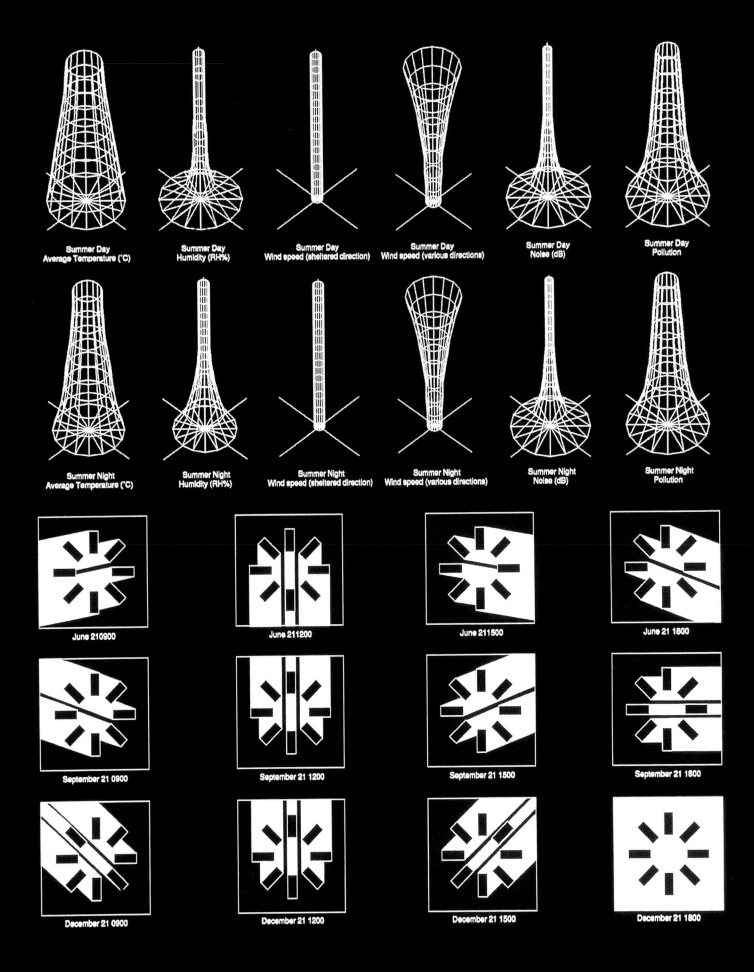

Summer Day
Average Temperature (°C)

Summer Day
Humidity (RH%)

Summer Day
Wind speed (sheltered direction)

Summer Day
Wind speed (various directions)

Summer Day
Noise (dB)

Summer Day
Pollution

Summer Night
Average Temperature (°C)

Summer Night
Humidity (RH%)

Summer Night
Wind speed (sheltered direction)

Summer Night
Wind speed (various directions)

Summer Night
Noise (dB)

Summer Night
Pollution

June 210900

June 211200

June 211500

June 21 1800

September 21 0900

September 21 1200

September 21 1500

September 21 1800

December 21 0900

December 21 1200

December 21 1500

December 21 1800

The Hong Kong Tower: three-dimensional plots of environmental conditions over the 1,000m height of the tower, and shadow drawings showing which buildings are in the shade for different sun positions

106

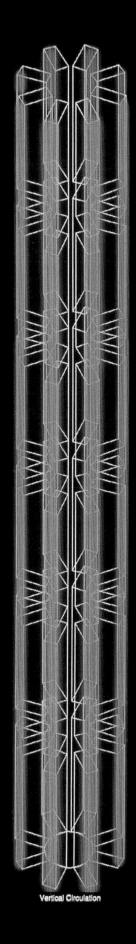

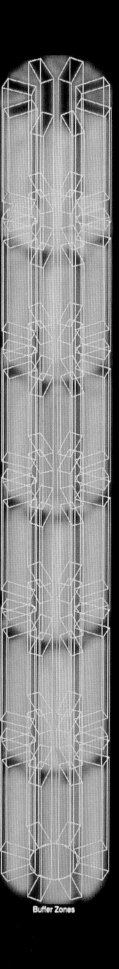

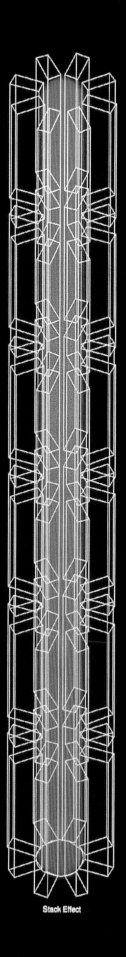

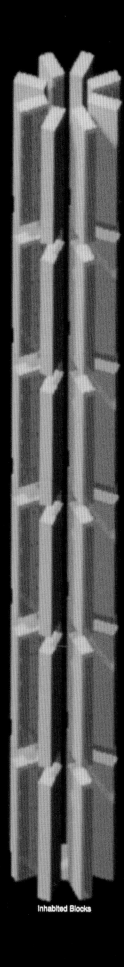

Vertical Circulation

Buffer Zones

Stack Effect

Inhabited Blocks

Vertical circulation; buffer zones; stack effect; inhabited blocks

STRUCTURAL SUBSTANCE OF COMPOSITE DETAILING

The iron bridge of Coalbrookedale was detailed as though it was made of timber, whilst today we see composite materials detailed as though they were steel. At present, the possibilities of detailing in composites have been unexplored, with the result that the structural form of composite construction is often bland, and fails to express the qualities of the material or the technical achievement. How we detail these composite connections is one of the essential challenges confronting structural engineers and architects today. The aim of this article is to explore methods by which details of structural significance may be developed.

Visual literacy

The understanding of architecture, and the excitement that can be generated by structure relies on visual literacy, itself based on codes and associations which vary across the globe. The modern visual literacy of structural form is now highly developed; we know that the strength and stiffness of a structural section does not depend upon the mass of the section, but on the effectiveness of its visual shape to transmit stress. An 'I' will always be stronger and stiffer than an 'H', whatever the material.

However, visual decoding is much more complex when the viewer is confronted by the numerous plates of Naum Gabo's *Head No 2*, as reading such a work requires a fundamental and fluent understanding of visual structural language, as well as an appreciation of the wealth of the symbolic vocabulary.

Despite initial preconceptions, structural engineering is not so different from sculpture, as both are ways of understanding reality. The main difference is not so much in the aims but the method. The engineer depends upon measurement and mathematical formulae to explain phenomena, whereas sculpture tends to be an intuitive and visual approach. Even these distinctions are not absolute: many a great engineer has worked intuitively and numerous sculptors have shown a rigorous intellectual approach in their work.

Structural substance

Whether we are looking at the creations of engineers or sculptors, we must be aware of the visual language; light, shape, colour, texture, lines, patterns, similarities, contrasts and movements. In engineering, visual literacy may be defined as the competence to illustrate structural substance by complementing physical function with a visual expression.

	Structural Function	Visual function
Purpose	Support, enclose, contain, shelter, shield	Comunicate information, express idea or attitude, convey feelings or mood, personality
Context	Loading, allowable stress and strain, stability, technology, economy, culture climate	spatial, perceptual, environment, cultural, social expectations
Materials	Earth, stone, metal wood, concrete, glass plastic, fabric	Visible spectrum
Elements	Slab, panel, beam girder, joists, column, post, tie, strut	Thick, thin, bold, slender, stiff, flexible
Attributes	Size, weight, shape, strenght, stiffness, cost, durability	Position, direction, brightness, size shape, texture, colour, surface, quality, duration
System	Arch, vault, shell, dome truss, frame, membrane	Proximity, closure, similarity, continuance, rhythm, movement
Joints	Bearing, friction, weld, cement, rivet bolt, pin, mortar, adhesive, node	Harmony, chaos, identify similarity, contrast, ambiguity
Criteria	Equilibrium, safety, durability, economy	Composition, legibility, expressiveness, coherence, order, balance, equilibrium, mobility

Contemporary techniques for expressing structural substance

The common denominator of structural and visual function is the ordering of materials within a consistent form. A structural form

2

3

1 *Amédee Bertault,* Auguste Rodin's Hand; *engineering and sculpture creating form out of formless matter*
2 *Cast iron detailed like timber, Coalbrookedale Bridge*
3 *Naum Gabo,* Head No 2

4

5

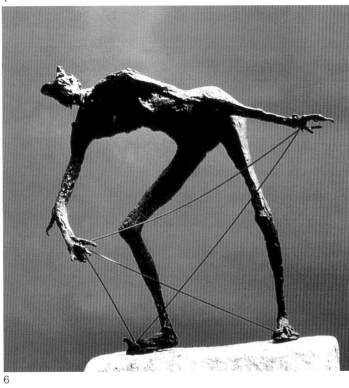

6

7

devolved solely from rational assessment, without passion and sensitivity, is only a topographical solution to a technical problem; whilst a structural form developed from emotional responses, without any real root in technology, will only be an isolated graph of an individual state of mind. Structural substance requires both, and there are basic principles that relate to a sculpture or to engineering:

Structure	Composition in space
Unity	Complete vision
Consistency	Clarity of expression

Admittedly, instruction about the techniques associated with sculpture – symbolising stability or movement – may seem out of context with the design of modern structural engineering, and the freedoms associated with sculpture may seem incompatible with the formulated disciplines of traditional structural design. Nevertheless, there are some design criteria associated with both the work of sculptors and engineers which assist in illustrating structural.

The suggestive power of structural substance of composite materials

Our eye senses not only colour but also data, which enables the brain to form images of the three-dimensional spatial characteristic of objects, allowing sensory judgement of symbolic content. We react primarily to:

Proportions	Dimentions of elements
Composition	The space between the elements
Contrast	The relationship between the elements (curves and straight lines)

In developing a detail in composites we understand its functional purpose, but it is much more difficult to define the emotional and spiritual aspects of its structural substance. We should once again involve ourselves in the 'Drama of Engineering', in its range from creating a secure enclosure with reassuring interlocking arches, to the uninhabitable projection of angular forms. Detailing in composites offers the opportunity of creating an appearance of a personality appropriate to its purpose and significance.

Composite form and detailing with symbolised harmony

The word harmony may be defined as a state of order, implying something which is aesthetically pleasing or visually stable, and is derived from the Greek work *harmos*, meaning a joint, and *harmozein*, to join together. With composites, we are involved in the physical and visual joining together of structural elements, such as beams, columns, ties and struts, with pins, knots and stitching. In as much as we are capable of assessing musical harmony instinctively, it may be possible to train our eyes to

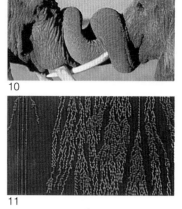
10

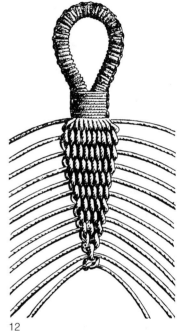
11

12

8

9

The theme of the human torso is one of the most frequent means of symbolising stability or movement
4, 5 The form of The Thinker *by Rodin has been developed to contain an inner force, whereas the iron connection of Brighton Pier clasps the forces between intercepting elements*
6, 7 The diagonal ties held by Richier's Devil with Claws *create forces in as much as the bracing at the Pompidou Centre accommodates them*
8, 9 The two angels in Lynn Chadwick's Winged Figure *represent our mechanical age in which the work bears witness to the art movement of the 60s. calculation, invention and understanding replaced the free play of the imagination, and the formal order of structural systems achieved aesthetic results – creating a constructive symbol of the aeroplane design technical revolution*
10 Interlocking elephant trunks
11 A pattern of dendrites, created by cellular automation with an asymmetric transition rule
12 Puddening an anchor ring

evaluate the visual harmonies of structures.

The presence or lack of these different aspects of structural substance reveals the professional touch of skilful detailing. They effect the overall impact of the composition, the feeling for the onlooker that everything is in its right place, that nothing could be added or taken away; the unmistakable completeness of symbolic content. Armed with these fundamental principles of form, the designer will find that he or she can see and correct many things that disturb the efficiency of the detail's geometry. A random grouping of composite elements will not produce a serviceable bridge, and neither will an unorganised collection of perceptual elements result in a coherent visual statement; only when the composite materials are properly joined and related to each other does the bridge become serviceable.

To our eyes the geometry of a bridge is seen as a complex arrangement of lines, shapes, volumes, masses, shadows and colours, which all seem incidental to the detail itself, yet all become a vital part in determining its value as a work of engineering. To some extent it is a good test of a 'satisfactory' detail that it composes well when seen from any direction, which means that it has the completeness of conception, as emphasised by Michelangelo in his work. Interestingly, the structural engineer Robert Maillart asserted: 'if the geometry of a structure looks right, it is right'.

There are several features which should be borne in mind when designing structure:

Simplicity: Simplicity is common to excellence in all the arts; it is elegance with economy of material. Just as in sculpture the most elegant solution may be achieved by simple gestures, the most economical solution in structural design may prove to be the best. Simplicity is not necessarily easy to achieve, as the impression of ease is usually the result of intensive skilful effort.

Necessity: Necessity is perhaps the key to harmony. How magnificent is the result if there is nothing in a detail, but that which is necessary. This is not a paradox. The mind is at rest in the acceptance of necessity, but is uneasy with the superfluous, the factitious.

Order: The principle of order is to avoid unnecessary accessories. The geometry should be so refined that one can neither remove nor add any element without disturbing the harmony of the whole. Order means clarity. Geometry with too many directions creates disquiet, confuses the observer and arouses disagreeable emotions; good order is achieved by limiting the directions of geometrical lines and edges.

We can also include the repetition of equal elements under the role of order. Repetition provides rhythm, which creates satisfaction. Yet too much repetition leads to monotony, so often encountered in 20th-century structures. The designer should interrupt its predictability and introduce some element of surprise.

The appropriate details of a composite connection are enhanced by the harmonies of simplicity, necessity and order; but the creation of originality requires tension between variety and similarity, and between complexity and order, which doubtlessly demands artistic skills. Designers should take note of the works of past and present sculptors who have been able to achieve fluidity, as well as the unexpected, within the order of a harmonious design.

Summary

Detailing of composite materials frequently lacks flair and imagination, failing to illustrate the qualities inherent in the material or the skill of their authors. The product is often merely a statement of the facts, unable to invoke the excitement, expectations, interest and even the admiration of craftsmanship.

Remember the delight, when as a child you built your first structure? To come near to this fundamental awareness of art, you need to sense and feel for a structural symbolic context, in terms of lines shapes, forms and colours. Like the Chinese artist of old, say a prayer and learn to be humble before the pencil touches the paper.

The authors would like acknowledge the contribution made by Douglas Broadley to the preparation of this article.

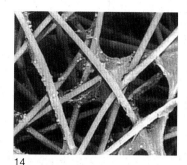

14

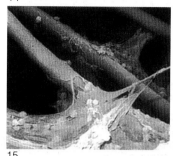

15

16

13 *Sketch development of a composite bridge*
14, 15, 16 *Scaffolding has been constructed to provide a template for formation of new tissue (shown enlarged, from above to below, x200, x500, x1000). The biodegradable plastic has been seeded with cells, which divide and assemble until they cover most of the structure. Eventually the plastic degrades leaving only tissue.*

ENGAGING PRE-ENGINEERING TECHNOLOGY IN CHONGQING, CHINA

Developing a dynamic dialogue between macro and micro scales in the production of a Sustainable Masterplan

Until now, mass housing has remained an albatross, impervious to any real advancements in engineering and design technology. As other forms of production have moved on, the housing industry has remained weighed down by its own particular set of construction conditions and traditions. The frustration of repeatedly encountering the same obstacles in its work on sustainable, conventionally conceived housing developments has encouraged Battle McCarthy to investigate more far-reaching solutions for pre-assembled housing units.

Prefabrication has the double advantage of bypassing substantial amounts of site work and the involvement of mediating agencies, such as developers, who can often compromise the end result both in terms of design and sustainability. There was, however, an even more far-sighted motivation for researching innovative technologies for pre-assembled homes than mere frustration with the status quo. As it stands, more than half of the world's population now live and work in cities. Even given the ever-increasing demand for urban accommodation and the shortage of suitable housing stock, there is at present no existing design and construction system capable of rising to the demographic challenge.

Battle McCarthy is proposing the proliferation of a wholly new sustainable building technology that could usher in a new era of residential, urban environmental building design with major global consequences. It is a system of pre-assembled housing that is set to transform 20th-century preconceptions of modular construction. Whereas in previous decades, prefabrication has been associated with the lowest common denominator of social housing and ultimately with 'failed' construction techniques, the proposed system is to be precision-engineered to a high standard and at a reasonable cost.

This should allow not only environmental building technology to infiltrate the construction industry in such a way that is inconcievable at present, but also ultimately, in a way that it will saturate the market unchallenged.

Though Battle McCarthy has been developing this building technology through its work on some of the largest housing schemes in Britain – such as the Greenwich Millennium Village and the Elephant and Castle in London – the next stage in its evolution has been dependent on its engagement on a project substantial enough to require a dedicated manufacturing base. (Within Europe, housing is not on a large enough scale to warrant the establishment of such a base.) However, the new housing construction programme in Western China, on which it has been invited to collaborate along with the Chongqing Construction Commission, Chongquing University and Hong Kong Polytechnic, has been set up to re-house a million people made homeless by the Three Gorges Dam project and the flooding of the Yangzte River. Entitled ECOS, this innovative scheme of industrial housing will produce precison-engineered and advanced IT-configured homes that will be applicable both locally and globally. For once it has been established, the ECOS's manufacturing base will export houses for a full range of international uses, including, for example, the provision of key workers' accommodation in London.

Four major factors make Chongqing ripe for the implementation of ECOS: the current and potential wealth of the region; the urgent need for a major construction programme; the government's concerns over the environmental impact of proposed construction; and the existence of a local shipbuilding industry with relevant skills for producing prefabricated housing units.

Schematic sketches by Battle McCarthy of the principles of a pre-engineered terrace house solution, which is to be developed for Chongqing in Western China.

CHONGQING MUNICIPALITY

Chongqing is a rapidly developing area based along the upper reaches of the Yangtze River. It is China's largest municipality, based at the heart of the Three Gorges project, which is the world's largest flood-control dam and hydro-electric project. The greater area is home to 30 million people with a population density of 367 people per square kilometre. Chongqing has a wealth of natural resources and provides a vast market potential for future development. A new infrastructure is beginning to evolve that will need to meet the investment demands and consumption needs of the millions of people who are now cultivating a high standard of living. The municipality has the resources and is ideally situated for the implementation of the ECOS system with population densities that make mass production a necessary element of the process.

Future Housing Demand in Chongqing

The Chinese Central and Regional Governments have conducted studies that reveal the need for Chongqing to undergo a major construction programme in order to meet future housing demands. It has been forecasted that this will require the construction of 61,500,000m² of space within the next five years. This increased demand has been caused by a number of factors, including the migration of people from rural to urban areas and the displacement and relocation of one million people due to the Three Gorges Dam Project

The space demands per person in Chongqing are also increasing. In 1978, it was 3m² per person and this doubled within 16 years to 6.3m² per person in 1994. It is now estimated to be 8m² per person and is expected to reach 12m² per person by 2005. The ECOS system can meet this challenge by providing a building system that can be erected quickly and efficiently, with the ability to respond to the growth in space demands as the quality of life in China grows.

The Environmental Impact of Proposed Construction

At present China produces only four times the amount of electricity generated in the UK for 20 times more people. A person living in China produces around 1 tonne of CO_2 per year, while an average American 'emits' 20 tonnes. These numbers could change dramatically in China as the standard of living increases and the demand for better lifestyles intensifies. The central and local governments recognise this and are extremely concerned about the environmental impact of the proposed construction programmes not only in Chongqing, but also throughout China. In response, they are establishing sustainability targets no different from

significant redevelopments in major Western cities. This will include environmental strategies that make use of available funding through Carbon Trading initiatives and that focus on construction quality, energy, water, waste and IT management. Chongqing is exploring industrialised housing – as is the UK – as a way to meet local as well as international environmental objectives. The ecologically and environmentally advanced designs of the ECOS system will help to establish the infrastructures necessary to address the short and long-term environmental issues that will arise. The design includes rainwater harvesting and recycling, low energy input during construction, zero CO_2 emission, renewable energy, effective waste management and recycling, low maintenance, high insulation and air tightness, demountable and reusable structures and services.

Industrialised Housing

Industrialised housing has become the development policy in Chongqing to replace poor quality traditional construction. It uses the same manufacturing techniques as the local shipbuilding industry which produces passenger liners – including cabin fit-out – as well as shops and major infrastructure and industrial components, such as bridges and manufacturing plant. Chongqing has the local resources to implement the housing construction programme but accepts the need to import international design expertise and appropriate equipment to adapt its shipbuilding industry. To this end, Battle McCarthy has developed the Scheme Design for a pre-engineered town-house system aimed at the middle-income and high-density inner-city market. The combination of the manufacturing techniques of China with the designs of Battle McCarthy will result in the precision-engineered mass production of large numbers of units. These numbers would never have been achievable in the West because the populations are less extreme. This provides the ideal opportunity to demonstrate the benefits of the ECOS system to the housing industry in the western world, where industrialised housing is not a financially viable option.

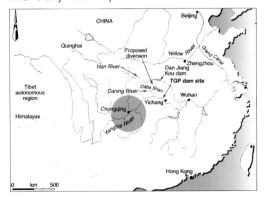

Map of Western China, showing Chongqing, the proposed site of ECOS. A housing project on a massive, unpredented scale, it can only be realised by using the pre-engineering technology that Battle McCarthy are helping to develop.

PRE-ENGINEERED SOLUTIONS

The pre-engineered town-house system is constructed from six stacked 'wet' units that incorporate kitchen and bathroom zones as well as a stair core. These are pre-commissioned and entirely manufactured off site with the floor and roof units. Everything is produced in a precision-engineering environment using low embodied energy recycled materials. All elements are delivered completed in the largest finished units and assembled on the site, where they create a full-span structure that allows for flexibility and incremental expansion.

Pre-engineered housing is environmentally streamlined with zero defects in order to maximise efficiency and achieve zero CO_2 emissions. The town house is also an Intelligent/Smart Home that possesses a computerised building control/management system and incorporates advanced features such as 'central locking' and home care or medical health monitoring.

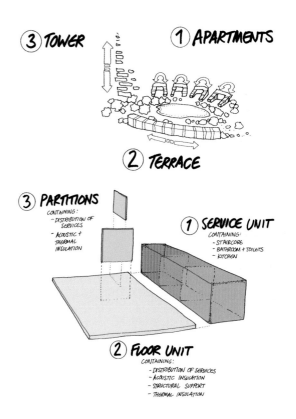

ABOVE: The three main elements of the pre-engineered house's structure. They are all delivered complete on site. CENTRE: The housing system allows for flexibility, incremental expansion and variation in building type. It can be used to construct higher rise housing and apartments, as well as terraced housing. RIGHT: The components that make up the largest finished unit of the pre-engineered house. Manufactured entirely off site, each house is constructed out of six 'wet units' that contain services and a stair core.

1. Primary frame

6. Doors

2. Secondary frame

7. Facade, Frame and Windows

3. Stairs

8. Plasterboard

4. Floor and Ceiling

9. External Envelope & Clip on Balconies

5. Services

JOINED-UP THINKING AND THE BENEFITS TO THE COMMUNITY

Quality and affordable IT-configured homes have obvious direct benefits for the housing industry, but in addition, the solution has far-reaching benefits such as:

Transportation – IT links to public transport

Education – IT lifetime learning

Health – Quality Environment

Retail – Centralised locking that provides controlled access

Social Security – Home-care facilities for the elderly and infirmed

Employment – Quality construction and dual-use homes

No longer can housing be isolated from the Government Departments of Health, Education, Transportation, Employment, Energy, Social Security and Environment. Housing, although a small government budget compared to other community needs, has a major influence on the performance of other departments. The Treasury has already made moves to escalate 'Best Practice' guidelines, which will be extended to include all benefits.

SUMMARY

The success of this partnership between Battle McCarthy and developers in China will provide a workable solution for growth in China as well as demonstrating to the house-building industry in the West that precision engineering is necessary to manufacture large numbers of pre-assembled homes. Such designs can then be applied to the increased urban development currently taking place in London and other international cities. The sustainable building techniques developed by Battle McCarthy will provide economic and 'best-value' benefits as well as 'future-proofing' the system for the expected developments in renewable energy systems.

Battle McCarthy recognises the value of the opportunities that global sustainability will bring to the housing industry and hope that this will soon be recognised by multi-nationals as low-energy industrial housing in China becomes a market opportunity both overseas and at home. In the near future, a superior industrialised home may be imported from Chongqing to provide a significantly better product than traditional housing, with all of the intelligent home facilities, at the same price as a minimum specification home in the UK. Ideally, a housing factory can be built on the outskirts of any major city, providing the necessary quality housing whenever it is needed.

Battle McCarthy is a visionary practice that realises the necessity for sustainable engineering design in architecture. The ECOS project represents a significant step in the realisation of a high quality and practical system for environmental housing. The practice has discovered the technology for saving the planet and preventing our own self-destruction. Now it will be applied on an unimaginable scale.

DELIVERING A SUSTAINABLE FUTURE

As designers and engineers of environments, our remit extends beyond the design of the building fabric itself and engages with the elements. We require a directed multidisciplinary and interdisciplinary approach, which creates a rich palette of tools to propose solutions for a sustainable future.

Unintegrated design wastes our precious energy, material and skill resources. No matter how efficiently we design each component of our built environment, we can only make real improvements through an integrated approach.

We need to re-evaluate and redefine understandings of value, in order to equip ourselves to respond to change and to reconsider how projects are measured as 'best value'.

The following examples are specific aspects of projects that allow us to discuss how we can start to deal with the complex nature of defining a basis for creative solutions for a sustainable future. These deal with elemental forces: wind, water, solar. Although the projects are not solely about these elements, they serve a useful purpose in highlighting how they have been used to produce an integrated solution.

Diagram demonstrating the relationship of multidisciplinary engineering criteria and elemental forces that can provide a rich platform to create exciting solutions towards a sustainable future.

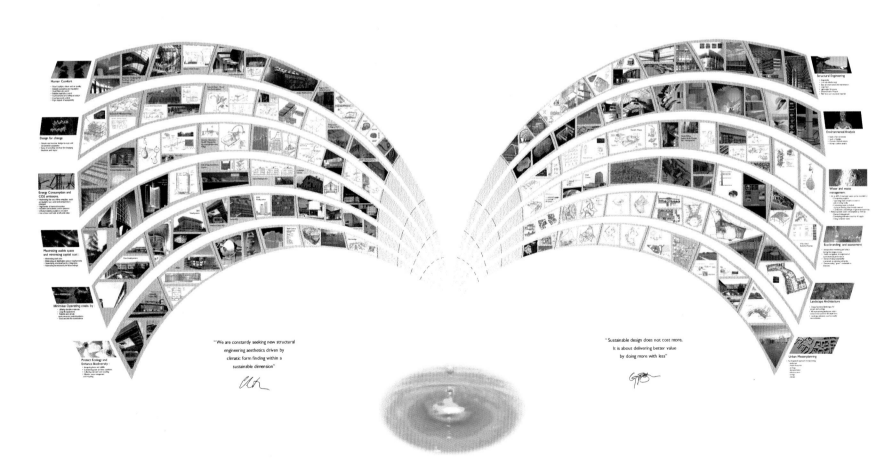

"We are constantly seeking new structural engineering aesthetics driven by climatic form finding within a sustainable dimension"

"Sustainable design does not cost more. It is about delivering better value by doing more with less"

Water as a Liquid Asset
Project: Rare Headquarters, Twycross, UK
Architect: Feilden Clegg Bradley Architects

The water cycle deals with two sources of water: the sky and the ground. The water is an asset as a form of potential and kinetic energy that can be used to provide 'warmth' or 'coolth'.

The rainwater is collected, filtered and treated, and is used within the functions of the building or to irrigate the landscape. The water proceeds to the lake and then into the ground. The lake provides evaporative cooling and light reflection as well as sound.

When the water is taken from the ground, there is a temperature difference that can be used to moderate the climate of the building. One method is to use the water for evaporating cooling. The building harmonises within this process, and forms a completion of the water cycle.

FROM ABOVE:
Model study of the site, to test orientation and massing and develop using prevailing winds to take advantage of passive technological design; Wind towers provide controllable natural ventilation

Wind-Powered Ventilation

Project: Haute Vallée School, Jersey, Channel
Islands
Architect: PLB Architects

We now have a much better understanding of
wind data from analysis of the air-travel industry
analytical data, wind tunnels and computer
analysis. These wind studies have been important in developing a possibility of an aerodynamic architecture.

Understanding of regional weather patterns and
microclimates allows us to design buildings
whose orientation and massing of form takes
advantage of wind as a natural resource for saving energy in terms of ventilation. Energy generation can also be provided by wind turbines.

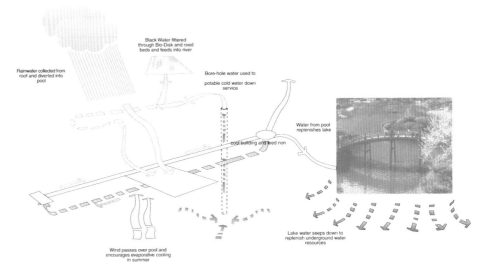

*TOP: Diagram showing the cycle of
water from the sky and the ground,
and how a building can harmonise
within this cycle.
RIGHT: Lake as a rainwater collector.
LEFT:Water channel within the landscaping around the building.*

Solar Heating

Project: Greenwich Millennium Village,
Greenwich Peninsula, London, UK
Architects: HTA/Ralph Erskine

Solar-enhanced design works at different
scales. The proposals for Greenwich Millennium
Village were developed by modelling solar and
view analysis. The solution was to create criteria
to enhance solar gain and river views, maximise
solar penetration, and optimise wind protection
– a strategy for facade design, planting and
landscaping.

This evolved the design into a series of court-
yards, modelled on the idea of the London
square, as a string of pearls around the park.
The massing of the development rises from the
south-west to the north to maximise river views
but also minimises overshadowing by taller
parts of the development.

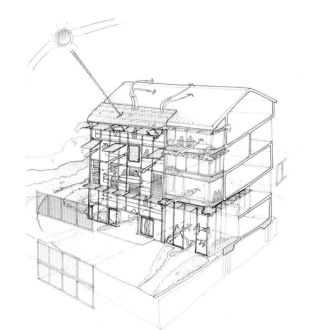

*ABOVE: Isometric drawing demon-
strating flexibility in facade design in
response to spatial adaptability and
environmental design.*
*CENTRE: Cross-section analysis, to
communicate to the design team the
overall concepts of solar utilisation.*
*BELOW: Model study of the Greenwich
Peninsula site, to test orientation and
massing and to develop and refine the
master-planning strategy.*

Precision Engineering
Zero Defects

Project: Elephant and Castle Redevelopment,
London, uk
Architects: kp Architects, Foster and Partners,
Ken Yeang, hta, Benoys

A precision-engineering approach creates and
adds value to a development. Previously, high
land costs were balanced against cheap construction with little regard for engineering performance, especially acoustic isolation, daylight
and adaptability. The redevelopment of the
Elephant and Castle is based on raising values
not only through environmental improvement but
also through the quality of construction.

We have an opportunity to bring value to a development, based on the quality of the engineered
solution. In order to bring this quality, a refine-
ment of the efficiency in how the elements of the
building are brought together is necessary.

The ecological aspects of a fit-for-purpose design
minimises waste, maximises quality and aids efficiency not only in the process of assembling a
building but also in its performance in use.

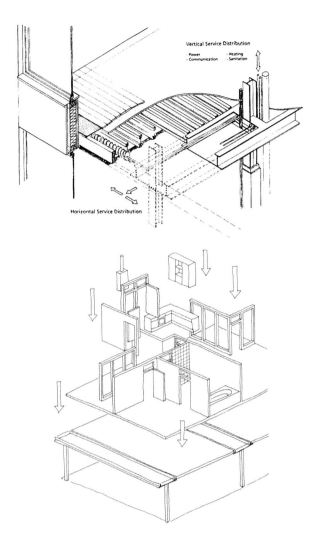

ABOVE: Isometric detail showing
the relationship of a coordinated
engineered solution of floors, superstructure, ceilings and external
envelope.
CENTRE: Prefabricated engineered
elements are modularised and co-
ordinated to minimise waste and
maximise speed of construction.
BELOW: Perspective sketch
showing overall master plan of the
Elephant and Castle area of London.

Delivering a Sustainable Future:
An Integrated Approach

Both sustainable urban master planning and building engineering require a wide variety of issues to be integrated in order to produce goals of sustainability. We need to look at holistic and integrated solutions for establishing a future that is sustainable.

The value of a built environment now extends beyond simplistic accounting of its financial value – an educated public demands not only quality but also social and environmental responsibility. The development of solutions arises out of the overlapping and integration of disciplines and expertise.

As we learn more about the possibilities of sustainable solutions, further work is required in producing intelligent interaction between urban master planning and building engineering.

We need to be able to think on a macro and a micro scale, considering the physical and non-physical, and redefining quality and value. Disciplines involved with the built environment need to understand, communicate and work with each other.

An integrated solution requires effective action. As the sustainable master planning and building technology evolves, a plan is needed for sustainable management. Establishing a community trust will ensure that the community will be run more efficiently and cost-effectively as a business. The trust will not only keep the local community, businesses and authorities as stakeholders, it will also involve the utility companies and building suppliers in a proactive steering group throughout design, construction and operation, thus meeting 'best value' targets.

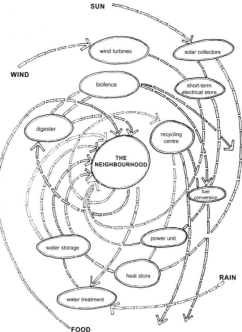

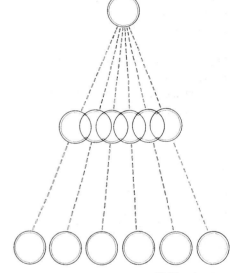

ABOVE: The diagram represents the possibility of establishing a single community trust responsible for the construction, operation and modification of a sustainable community in association with utilities and building suppliers.
CENTRE: Diagram illustrating complex processes involved in creating dynamic relationships between the input and output from an inclusive sustainable development.
BELOW: Both sustainable urban master planning and building engineering require a wide variety of issues to be integrated in order to produce goals of sustainability.

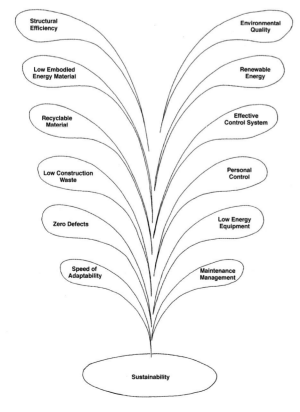

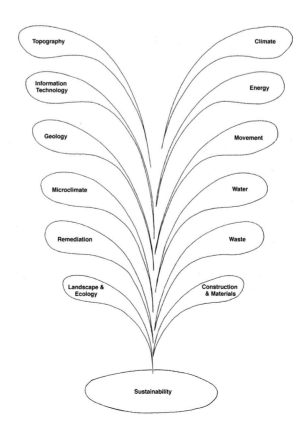

List of projects undertaken by Battle McCarthy since their iception

OFFICES & COMMERCIAL

Battle McCarthy Landscape Architects
Cable & Wireless Surrey Quays London, UK
Environmental Engineering and
Landscape Architecture

Kohn Pedersen Fox Architects
Endesa Headquarters, Madrid, Spain
Structure and Services Design

Studio Gang O'Donell Architects
Tag Warehouse, Goose Island Chicago, USA
Environmental Engineering

Damond Lock Grabowski & Partners
I Paternoster Row, London, UK
Environmental Services and Analysis

RH Partnership Architects
Velux Southern Regional Offices Design
Competition
Environmental Strategy and Services Engineering

Millennium Tower
Nairobi, Kenya
Building Services and Natural Wind
Ventilation Analysis

Nicholas Grimshaw & Partners
Toyota Headquarters, UK
Environmental and Landscape Design

Sauerbruch Hutton Architects
New Central Towers, Brussels, Belgium
Refurbishment of the Central Tower in Brussels

German Department of the Environment /
UBA, Dessau, Germany
Environmental, Landscape and Structural Design

Kohn Pedersen Fox Associates
World Trade Centre, Amsterdam, The Netherlands
Environmental and Urban Strategy Design

Alsop & Störmer Architects
Düsseldorf Hafen
Environmental Services Design for a
Port Development

Buschow Henley Architects
HHCL Headquarters
Structural and Environmental Engineering

Hijjas Kasturi SDN Architects
Sime Darby Headquarters, Kuala Lumpur,
Malaysia
Structural and Environmental Design

Pringle Richards Sharrat Architects
Bastion House
Structural and Environmental Design

Whinney Mackay Lewis Partnership
Novello House, Wardour Street, London, UK
Structural and Environmental Design

International Headquarters for Pilkington Plc
Building Services

Terry Farrell & Partners
D - building, Seoul, South Korea
Environmental Analysis, Structure and
Services Engineering

Delta Architects
Budget Rent - A - Car Headquarters,
London Heathrow, UK
Structure and Services Design

Alsop & Störmer Architects
Maison Europa, Geneva, Switzerland
Structure and Environmental Services Design

Hijjas Kasturi SDN Architects
Bandar Tasik Selatan Transport Interchange,
Kuala Lumpur, Malaysia
Environmental and Structural Design

Harper Mackay Architects
M&C Saatchi Headquarters, Golden Square,
London, UK
Refurbishment Project

Feilden Clegg Architects
New Headquarters for RARE Ltd , Twycross
Multi - disciplinary including Structure, Services
and Landscape Design

BUJ Architects
County Hall, Adington Street Block
Structural, Environmental and Building Services

Kohn Pedersen Fox Architects
House of Representatives, Nicosia, Cyprus
Multi - Disciplinary Engineering Design

Jersey Powerhouse, Jersey Electricity Company
Refurbishment of the Queens Road Powerstation

Provinciehuis, The Netherlands
Multi-Disciplinary Engineering Design

T. R. Hamzah & Yeang Architects
Bonia Headquarters, Johor Baharu, Malaysia
Multi-Disciplinary Engineering Design

Kohn Pedersen Fox Architects
Centre International Rogier, Martini Tower
Brussels, Belgium
Environmental and Building Services Design

RH Partnership Architects
Ionica Headquarters Building, St Johns College,
Cambridge
Environmental Design and Structural Engineering

Sauerbruch Hutton Architects
GSW Headquarters Building , Berlin, Germany
Structural & Environmental Design

CULTURAL

Whinney Mackay Lewis
Maitreya Buddha, Bodhgaya, India
Multi-Disciplinary Engineering including
Structural, Services and Landscape Design

Henning Larsens of Tegnestue
Danish Design Centre, Copenhagen,
Denmark
Environmental Services Design

John McAslan & Partners
Commonwealth Institute, London, UK
Environmental and Structural Design

Alsop & Störmer Architects
Royal Society of British Sculptors
Structural and Environmental Design

Levitt Bernstein
Salway Performing Arts Centre
Environmental Services Design

John McAslan & Partners
The Great Room: Royal Society of Arts
London, UK

Environmental and Services Engineering
refurbishment

Alan Baxter & Associates
Temple of the Vedic Planetarium,
Mayapur, India
Environmental Engineering Strategy

RHWL
Gresham School Theatre, Norfolk, UK
Structural Design and Construction of a new
300 seat theatre

RHWL Architects
Sadlers Wells Theatre, Rosebery Avenue
London, UK
Mechanical and Electrical Services Engineering

Alsop & Störmer Architects
Tate Gallery Bankside, London, UK
Environmental Design Analysis,
Competition entry

Andrew Wright Associates
Tibetan Retreat Holy Island, Arran,
Scotland, UK
Multi-Disciplinary Engineering, self-sustaining
development for Buddhist community

COMMUNITY AND EDUCATION

T. R. Hamzah & Yeang Architects
The University of Nottingham, Malaysia
Urban Masterplanning & Building Technology

Terry Farrell & Partners
Computer Laboratory Building University
of Cambridge, UK
Multi-Disciplinary Engineering

YRM Associates
New International and Commonwealth
University, Malaysia
Structural, Environmental and Urban Design

Alsop & Störmer Architects
Central St. Martins College of Art
London, UK
Environmental Analysis and
Services Engineering

Pringle Richards Sharrat Architects
Middlesex University Real Tennis Courts,
Middlesex, UK
Structural and Environmental Design

Michael Hopkins & Partners
Nottingham University Campus,
Nottingham, UK
Landscape Design

Chris Wilkinson Associates
Latymer School Performing Arts Centre
Environmental and Structural Engineering

National Innovation Centre
Structural and Environmental Building
Services Engineering

Alsop & Störmer Architects
Peckham Library and Media Centre,
Peckham, UK
Building Services

Cowgatehead Library, Edinburgh, UK
Environmental, Structure and
Services Design

RHWL
  Gresham School Theatre, Norfolk, UK
  Structural Design and Construction of a
  new 300 seat Theatre

Gruntuch & Ernst
  Hellersdorf Kindergarten, Berlin, Germany
  Structural and Services Design for a
  Special Needs school

Terry Farrell & Partners
  Keele University, Stoke-on-Trent, UK
  Detailed Design and Feasibility Studies for
  a renewable energy

Architecture PLB
  Winchester College of Art, Winchester, UK
  Services Engineering

  Eilenburgerstraße School Berlin, Germany
  Structural and Environmental Services Design

URBAN DESIGN

Richard Rogers Partnership
  Piana di Castello, Florence, Italy
  Urban Design

Tower 151 Architects
  Zagrebacka Banka, Zagreb, Croatia
  Environmental Services Design

Kohn Pedersen Fox Associates
  Groningen Zuid Oost - Zuid Plein, Amsterdam,
  The Netherlands
  Environmental and Urban Strategy

Terry Farrell & Partners
  Cambourne New Town, Cambridge, UK
  Detail Design and Feasibility Studies for a
  Renewable Energy System

Richard Rogers Partnership, Future Systems
  Solar City, Linz, Austria
  Structural, Services & Passive Solar Design

PRIVATE HOUSES

Mark Fisher Architects
  Concept Housing Design
  Structural and Environmental Design

Asef Gottesman Architects
  Litmore Shaw House, Ibstone, Uk
  Structural and Landscape Design

John Browning Associate Architects
  81 Highgate West Hill, London, UK
  Structural and Building Services

Matthew Priestman Architects
  9 Endlesham Road
  Structural and Environmental Strategy

Circus Architects
  No. I Summers Street, London, UK
  Structural Design

Matthew Priestman Architects
  Private House at Nant - Y - Glas - Dwr, Cusop
  Environmental, Building Services and Structural
  Engineering

Sheppard Robson
  Parkshot House, Richmond, UK
  Structure and Services Engineering Scheme
  Design

RESIDENTIAL HOUSING

Battle McCarthy
  Ecos, Pre - Engineered Terrace House System
  Consulting Engineers and Landscape
  Architects, overall Scheme Design

S333 Architects
  Living in the City, Competition Submission,
  London, UK
  Structural Concept

Harper Mackay Architects
  Goswell Road Live/ Work Space, London, UK
  Environmental and Structural Design

Co. Karlese van der Meer Architecten
  Europan 5, Kop Van Zuid, The Netherlands
  Multi-Disciplinary Consulting Engineers for this
  competition winning scheme

Heiko Luhas with Ulrike & Joachim Staudt
  Pankow Housing Competition, Berlin, Germany
  Sustainable Energy, Ecology and Infrastructure
  Schematics

Architecture Bureau
  Verde Heights, Kualar Lumpur, Malaysia
  Ecological Landscaping of Residential
  Development

Neutelings Riedijk Architechten
  Hague Housing
  Environmental Analysis, Structural and Services
  Engineering

de Architekten Cie
  Karlshorst Housing Scheme, Germany
  Short-listed Competition Entry

ENVIRONMENTAL & SUSTAINABLE
MASTERPLANNING

Ove Arup Partners & TM2
  Elstow New Settlement
  Masterplanning, Urban and Landscape Design

Kohn Pedersen Fox Associates
  Airport Gardens, Brussels, Belgium
  Building Services Engineering, Environmental
  Analysis and Urban Design

Baker Brown Mackay, HTA Architects
  Norfolk Park Sheffield, Sheffield, UK
  Environmental Design, Analysis and
  Masterplanning

Ralph Erskine Architects
  Greenwich Millennium Village, London, UK
  Structural, Environmental Analysis, Landscape
  and Urban Design

Nicholas Pearson Architects
  Blackwall Point, Greenwich, UK
  Ecological Design

  Eastern Riverwall, Greenwich Peninsular
  Masterplan
  Ecological and Environmental Advice Report

Richard Rogers Partnership
  Parc BIT, Mallorca, Spain
  Sustainable Masterplanning

Richard Rogers Partnership
  Tel Aviv Peninsula, Israel, Asia
  Sustainable Ecological Masterplanning and
  Urban Design

Future Systems
  The Earth Centre Environmental
  Masterplanning
  Environmental Masterplanning

Plincke Leaman Browning Architects
  D' Hautree School, Jersey, UK
  Multi - disciplinary including Structure, Services
  and Landscape Design

INFRASTRUCTURE

Cartwright Pickard
  Living in the City, Bishopsgate Village, UK
  Sustainable Energy, Ecology and Infrastructure
  Schematics

Terry Farrell & Partners
  Inchon International Airport Transportation
  Centre, Korea
  Environmental Design

IHeiko Lukas, Ulrike Lukas & Joachim Staudt
  Pankow Housing Competition
  Buch district of Berlin, Germany
  Sustainable Energy, Ecology and Infrastructure
  Schematics

Ideias Do Futuro
  De Rossio Station, Lisbon, Portugal
  Light Environmental Refurbishment of Existing
  Railway Station

JE · ECS
  Jersey Airport
  In Association with Jersey Energy and
  Environmental Control

Terry Farrell & Partners
  Barreiro Ferry Terminal

BRIDGES & STRUCTURAL

Terry Farrell & Co. Architects
  Hungerford Bridge Pedestrian Link
  Competition
  Environmental and Structural Design

T.R. Hamzah & Yeang Architects
  Super Mines Exhibition Golf Canopy, Malaysia
  Structural Design for a roof over a golf course
  driving range

Hijjas Kasturi SDN Architects
  Atrium Roof: SIDC Headquarters, Kuala
  Lumpur, Malaysia
  Environmental and Structural Design

  Poole Harbour Crossing
  Environmental and Structural Design

  Ideisa do Futuro's Composite Bridge - Expo '98
  in Lisbon, Portugal
  Consulting Engineers

PORTABLE & LIGHTWEIGHT
STRUCTURES

  European Union Pavilion Roof Canopy
  Environmental and Structural Design

Jacobs Architekten BV
  Skoda Showroom for Pon Mobiel BV, Leusdan,
  The Netherland
  Environmental Services Design

Hijjas Kasturi Architects
Kedah Arena, Malaysia
Environmental and Structural Design

Imagination
Siemens Portable Exhibition Truck
Structural and Services Engineers

Circus Architects
Mobile Cinema
Consulting Engineers and Structural Concept

Alsop & Störmer Architects
Bradwell Exhibition Centre
6000m ≈ demountable exhibition enclosure

Battle McCarthy
Orange Competition Ecological
Telecommunication Points
Landscape and Ecology competition entry

HIGH-RISE / TALL BUILDINGS

Dubus Richez Architects
Malaysia Airlines Headquarters Renovation,
Kuala Lumpur, Malaysia
Environmental and Structural Design

T. R. Hamzah & Yeang Architects
Exhibition Tower, Singapore
Environmental Design and
Structural Concepts

Wawasan and JMP Consultants Ltd.
Linear City, Kuala Lumpur, Malaysia
In collaboration with Battle McCarthy

T. R. Hamzah & Yeang Architects
UMNO Tower, Malaysia
Environmental Design

Terry Farrell & Co. Architects
Kowloon Station Eco Tower Masterplan
Economic Feasibility Study for Environmental
and Energy Assessment

Sheppard Robson Architects
Murr Tower, Beirut, Lebanon
Environmental Services Design

T. R. Hamzah & Yeang Architects
Haikou Towers
Environmental Services and Structural
Engineers

RETAIL

Alsop & Störmer Architects
C/Plex, West Bromwich, West Midlands, UK
Building Services and Environmental Analysis

Kuhne Architects
Bluewater Mall, Kent, UK
Strategic Engineering Design including Models
and CFD Analysis used for optimum
day-lighting and natural ventilation

Holmes Wright Partnership
British Rail Proteus Retail Unit for Newcastle,
Station, UK
Structural Cladding Communication and
Services Design

MEDICAL CENTRES

Douglas Stephens Partnership
Regents Park Medical Centre
Wind Tower Design for Environmental Control

**Yolles Partnership, Rybka Smith Ginsler,
Cambridge Research, Imperial College,
Exeter Energy Unit, Bristol Aeronautics
Department**
St. Mary's Medical Centre, Isles of Scilly
Structural, Services, Day-lighting and Acoustics,
Wind, Energy and Wind Ventilation -
in association with Battle McCarthy

LEISURE

Mark Braun
Niedersachen Stadium, Hamburg, Germany
Structural design for new stadium

Andrew Yeoman & John Kramer
International Health Club, Kuwait, Asia
Multi-Disciplinary Engineering including
Structure, Services and Landscape Design

Troughton McAslan
Putney Boat House, Imperial College Rowing
Club, London, UK
Structural and Services Design of a new
University boat house

Suria Eksklusif Ngiom Partnership
Jerai International Park, Malaysia
Structure, Environmental and Urban Design

Projects undertaken by Guy Battle and Christopher
McCarthy whilst at **OVE ARUP & PARTNERS**

Massimiliano Fuksas Architects
Candie Saint Bernard Sports Complex, France
Structural Engineering

T. R. Hamzah & Yeang Architects
Guthrie Pavilion, Malaysia
Structural Engineering

Alsop & Lyall Architects
Hamburg Ferry Terminal, Hambury, Germany
Building Engineering

Terry Farrell Partnership
Lee House Redevelopment, London Wall St, UK
Multi-Disciplinary Engineering including
Structural Design

Alsop & Störmer Architects
Marseille Town Hall, France
Building Engineering

John McAslan & Partners Architects
Max Mara Fashion Headquarters,
Reggio Emilia, Italy
Concept Structural Engineering to Phase I of
Competition

Mines Exhibition Hall, Malaysia
Structural Engineering

Foster & Partners
Renault Centre, Swindon, UK
Building Engineering

Trevor Dannatt Architects
Riyadh Diplomatic Quarter Sports Club
Structural Engineering

Seville Expo '92
Structural Engineering

T. R. Hamzah & Yeang Architects
Taichung Civic Centre, Taiwan
Multi-Disciplinary Engineering including
Structural, Services and Urban Design

Telecommunications Tower, Singapore
Structural Engineering

Terry Farrell & Partners Architects
The Peak, Hong Kong
Structural Engineering